Jenny's passion to help those who suffer from depression emerges from her personal journey. Her response springs from the Word of God. This book is Word-filled, balanced, and filled with warmth and encouragement. I am excited to see this new and powerful tool available.

—LARRY STOCKSTILL
BETHANY WORLD PRAYER CENTER
BATON ROUGE, LOUISIANA

It is so refreshing to finally see a book that focuses on a "real" cure for depression and anxiety. Jenny's heartfelt book is full of valuable tools and insights to help hurting souls find freedom in our Lord and Savior Jesus Christ. As a professional counselor and someone who has struggled with depression, I have been waiting for a resource that walks you step by step through a journey of healing and wholeness as Jenny's book so eloquently does. Jenny's personal struggle gives you a sense that she is walking alongside you as you heal. I am elated that she has chosen to write this book.

—BONNIE P. ROBERTS, LPC
WELLSPRING CHRISTIAN CLINIC
BIRMINGHAM, ALABAMA

Jenny is a dear friend and an amazing woman after God's own heart. This is not just a book but also a reflection of her own journey to spiritual and emotional healing. We have walked the steps in this book with women in a small group setting, and we have seen God move to heal soul wounds and change lives. I highly recommend this book, as it focuses on the only way to find true healing—by seeking God, our Creator and Healer.

—Tonya Nash, LPC, RPT
Counselor supervisor, Hillcrest Hospital
Birmingham, Alabama

This factual, God-inspired, life-changing book is an affirmation of hope and comfort for anyone who suffers from the emotional pain of depression. It reminds us that God will not only see us through life's challenges, but as we embrace the truths within these pages, He will also lovingly restore hope and joy to our lives.

—Marilyn Sampson
Praying With Passion Ministries
Birmingham, Alabama

FREEDOM FROM DEPRESSION

JENNY SWINDALL

CHARISMA
HOUSE

Most CHARISMA HOUSE BOOK GROUP products are available at special quantity discounts for bulk purchase for sales promotions, premiums, fund-raising, and educational needs. For details, write Charisma House Book Group, 600 Rinehart Road, Lake Mary, Florida 32746, or telephone (407) 333-0600.

FREEDOM FROM DEPRESSION by Jenny Swindall
Published by Charisma House
Charisma Media/Charisma House Book Group
600 Rinehart Road
Lake Mary, Florida 32746
www.charismahouse.com

Unless otherwise noted, all Scripture quotations are from the Holy Bible, New International Version. Copyright © 1973, 1978, 1984, International Bible Society. Used by permission.

Scripture quotations marked ASV are from the American Standard Bible.

Scripture quotations marked ESV are from the Holy Bible, English Standard Version. Copyright © 2001 by Crossway Bibles, a division of Good News Publishers. Used by permission.

Scripture quotations marked KJV are from the King James Version of the Bible.

Scripture quotations marked NKJV are from the New King James Version of the Bible. Copyright © 1979, 1980, 1982 by Thomas Nelson, Inc., publishers. Used by permission.

Scripture quotations marked NLT are from the Holy Bible, New Living Translation, copyright © 1996, 2004, 2007. Used by permission of Tyndale House Publishers, Inc., Wheaton, IL 60189. All rights reserved.

Library of Congress Cataloging-in-Publication Data:
An application to register this book for cataloging has been
submitted to the Library of Congress.
International Standard Book Number: 978-1-62136-228-9
E-book ISBN: 978-1-62136-229-6

While the author has made every effort to provide accurate
telephone numbers and Internet addresses at the time of
publication, neither the publisher nor the author assumes any
responsibility for errors or for changes that occur after publication.

AUTHOR'S NOTE: Some names, places, and identifying
details with regard to stories in this book have been changed
to help protect the privacy of individuals who may have had
similar experiences. The illustrations may consist of composites
of a number of people with similar issues and names and
circumstances changed to protect their confidentiality. Any
similarity between the names and stories of individuals described
in this book to individuals known to readers is purely coincidental.

First edition

13 14 15 16 17 — 9 8 7 6 5 4 3 2 1
Printed in the United States of America

This book is dedicated to my little brother, Brian Christopher Evans, who took his own life on April 26, 2011, at age twenty-nine. Brian was a brilliant, loving man who found the Lord in 2008 after realizing that he needed Jesus in his life. My mom had the glorious privilege of walking Brian through the sinner's prayer. Within these pages are all the things I wish I could have shared with him before he left this earth. After Brian went to heaven, I began writing late into the nights, compelled forward by my broken heart. I have typed through streams of tears and have leaned on Jesus to create this book. I pray that out of my pain and triumph you may find the freedom and love you are searching for in the arms of Jesus. Brian would have been so very proud of me. One day he and I will embrace again, and our joy will be complete.

Brian, this is for you. I love you.

CONTENTS

ACKNOWLEDGMENTS

L ET ME BEGIN by first giving thanks to Jesus for setting me free from the depths of depression and anxiety so that I could share the way of freedom with others. Jesus is my best friend, and it is an honor that He would allow me to serve Him in this way.

To my husband, Kevin, thank you for your boundless love and for being a man who adores Jesus. You are a treasured gift, and I am thankful for you each and every day.

Thank you to my parents, who told me that anything is possible, no matter what crazy idea I came up with next. Dad, you make me feel like a princess every day, and Mom, your advice guides my life in more ways than you know.

To my little brother, Michael, you are becoming such a wonderful man, and I am so proud of all you have accomplished.

To Maureen Eha and the entire Charisma House family, I will always be so very thankful that you would take a chance on this first-time author. And to my editor, Adrienne Gaines, and everyone who worked on this book—it's as if you knew my thoughts and were able to articulate them better than me sometimes! You made this project sing.

Finally, to my brother, Brian, whose home is in heaven now—I have planted your life as a seed in the kingdom garden, and I expect the blossoms of your life and our story to bloom throughout the earth every time I write, minister, and love others in the name of Jesus. I am thankful that we had you here for twenty-nine years, but I look forward to sharing eternity with you.

PREFACE

I N THE COMING pages you will find a resource that I hope
will encourage and bring freedom to those who are hurting
from depression. This is not a self-help book; it is more like a
"Jesus-help" book, because it was written for people who are
desperate to find a way out of depression and who know that
the Lord is their hope for freedom. If you've suffered from
depression in the past or have a friend struggling with depression, this book is for you too. And while women especially
may relate to my journey through depression, this is a guide
for anyone looking for a path to lasting healing and wholeness.

I am not a counselor, a psychologist, or a medical doctor.
This book is not meant to replace the advice of those professionals in their respective fields but simply to work alongside
them and to complement any therapies that you may already
be receiving. As you walk through this study, continue to seek
treatment through professionals, and always consult with your
doctor about starting or stopping any of your medications.

It is important to seek guidance from professionals, but I
believe it is also important to seek out what the Lord has to
say concerning depression. The Scripture has much to tell us
about this subject, and this book will give you specific scriptures and principles to help strengthen your faith. It is my
prayer that as you journey toward healing from depression,
you will see all of God's promises over your life come to pass.

This book was intended to be read over a period of twelve
weeks, one chapter each week—each week, another chapter,
another move of God in your life. Go slowly. I would rather

you savor each nugget of wisdom, each healing scripture, and each week's assignment than fly through the words and fail to see any real restoration in your life.

Holy Scripture is used each step of the way to point you to the Lord's heart for you. As you digest the words of the Lord, His peace will begin to settle into the wounds of your soul. When a scripture leaps off the page at you, copy or highlight it. Read and re-read the verses in this book. Look them up in your Bible; tape them to your mirror; keep them in your car. Make these verses the song of your spirit—your *freedom song*.

I also encourage you to get a notebook to record your responses to the reflection questions and exercises in the Dig Deeper sections at the end of each chapter. These exercises are designed for you to put into practice the principles you will be studying. Simply reading the book without spending time on the exercises will provide only marginal benefit for you. I have taught this material to scores of people who have battled depression, and over and over I have seen that those who find the most healing are the ones who take the time to ask themselves the tough questions and to apply the lessons in their own lives.

There are a great many layers to wade through in seeking freedom from depression, and each layer of breakthrough draws upon the one before it. You may walk successfully through one step only to find weeks or months later that you need to revisit it. *This plan is meant to be worked and reworked as you have need.* The more time you spend on the exercises listed at the end of each chapter, the more breakthrough you will see. Be fearless in pressing toward wholeness by putting each principle you discover into practice. It is worth it.

This book works well in a small-group format. Having other believers around you with whom you can talk through the details of this study is a great benefit. I encourage you to also watch the videos I have created to accompany each chapter. These can be viewed individually or within a small-group setting. You can find these videos at www.jennyswindall.com along with some other great resources that can be used for small-group Bible studies.

Whether you are a brand-new Christian, someone interested merely in a Christian approach to mental health, or a Bible-study leader, the Lord has something to say to you. Jesus died to bring freedom to all who are in chains. May you come to know complete freedom from depression through Jesus Christ.

MY JOURNEY TO HEALING

I will walk about in *freedom*, for I have
sought out your precepts.

—Psalm *119:45, emphasis added*

REMEMBER THE DAY so clearly. I have replayed that warm
afternoon many times in my heart. I would like to be able
to say that this was the day that everything changed, when
my battle finally ended, but it was actually the day my healing
began.

I was in my sophomore year of college in Auburn, Alabama.
At this point in my life I was completely enchained by the
heavy weights of depression and anxiety. It is a little odd for
me to tell this story, because I almost feel as if I am telling the
tale of another girl. I have to make myself remember those
days, because I am so changed now that I barely recognize the
scared, hopeless college kid that I was.

That spring day was so pretty—a day for enjoying the walk
to class and the beautiful outdoors. I was wearing jeans and
a yellow T-shirt. I had a few minutes before class, so I went
behind the biology building and slid down on the grass. With
my back against a tree, I waited there by the back door, staring
into the perfect sky.

By that second semester of my second year of college I was
totally consumed with this cancerous thing called depression.
I was barely making it to class, barely making it through the

day, barely hanging on to God. I bet some of you know just where I was that day. As I sat there on the ground, I started pouring my heart out to God, crying tears I was not proud of. I remember telling the Lord, "I am stuck inside this pit, and I cannot climb out of it, no matter what I do. If You do not come and get me out, I will remain here forever." I meant every word.

Again and again I had tried to climb out on my own. I had begged and prayed for God to get me out, and yet I remained under bondage. I knew I had no hope on my own. As I sat alone behind that building, looking up at the hot blue sky and telling God that I could not go on, unexpectedly the Lord spoke back to me.

I have heard from the Lord since I was young, but this day His voice was so clear it startled me. I had been watching a cloud float lazily across the sky, and I was so halted by the Lord's voice that I did not look back up again until He had finished speaking. To the best of my memory He said to me, "Daughter, just as those clouds have been moving across the sky, so will I move in your life. If you just glance at the clouds, you do not notice them moving. But if you look at them and then back again after some time, you can see that the cloud has surely moved. I am at work, even when you cannot see anything moving. Just as I move the clouds, I will remove this depression from your life."

And just as He had said, when I glanced back up at the sky, sure enough, that cloud I'd been watching had made a major move across that sky. And this is how I came to be healed.

The Lord fulfilled the promise He made to me that afternoon. I would love to say that I saw an instant blessing, but God remained true to His analogy. My complete healing took place over time in a million little blessings. But His promise to me was made complete, and I am happy to say that years have passed without any storm clouds forming in my life. I was made whole again by an amazing God who loves me so much that He rescued me from the pit of depression.

This book is not meant to merely encourage you with God's promise to move the clouds in your life. I hope it will challenge you to ask Him to come to your rescue and to be a vessel He can work through. Take my hand and walk with me as we talk about the Lord's goodness. Complete the assignments with your whole heart, and pray through the suggested prayers and scriptures. It is the Lord's will that you be made whole through Jesus. Go ahead and make the decision to choose God's Word over your own ways. Open your heart to healing, for it will please the Father. Be reminded that the Father always chooses freedom for His kids—it is we who sometimes do not choose it for ourselves.

Jesus was sent to "bind up the brokenhearted, to proclaim freedom for the captives and release from darkness for the prisoners" (Isa. 61:1). Let freedom begin.

Chapter 1

THE GREAT THIEF

I pour out my complaint before him; before him
I tell my trouble. When my spirit grows faint
within me, it is you who know my way.

—Psalm 142:2–3

I HAVE DEDICATED THIS book to my brother, because his
sudden death was the catalyst that caused me to begin
writing this book. But the Lord had actually called me to
write about healing from depression about four years before
he took his life. My husband, Kevin, and I were in Tennessee
attending a ministry conference, and since we had some time
between sessions, we decided to wander into a Christian
bookstore and browse. I am good at browsing—most women
are. I don't have to buy anything in a store to enjoy being
there. Of course, my husband likes stores about as much as
he likes a trip to the dentist. But we had an hour free, so
we settled into our favorite sections of the store and went to
work wasting time.

For some reason the idea of looking at books on emotional
healing seemed to pique my interest. I had long been healed of
my own depression by this time, but I wanted to see what was
out there for people who were suffering in silence as I once
had been. After a thorough search in the giant chain Christian
bookstore, I found two books on depression. Only two!

One in ten Americans is on an antidepressant,[1] and another study found that roughly one in ten women not being hospitalized for mental health complaints is on antidepressants.[2] I knew that churches didn't talk a lot about depression and anxiety, but seeing the lack of available materials on those subjects really drove that point home for me. So I bought the two books I had found, and at the hotel that night I started reading. The thing I discovered was that neither of the authors had ever battled depression personally. A counselor had written one book, and the other author was a medical doctor. Both books were informative, but they were clinical.

The limitation in these books was that both authors could describe depression only through their patients' eyes. Because the authors had never been in my shoes, I found that neither of them could fully empathize with their readers and thus maintained a very matter-of-fact approach. Both books described treatment plans, medication options, various kinds of depression, and so on, but they completely avoided the larger issue of spiritual health and wholeness that must be addressed along with physical well-being.

Of course, doctors, counselors, and medicines are all good aids (in fact, I think they are very good aids—*do* go see a specialist to get help), but if those alone worked perfectly, then depression would be obsolete. Ultimately a clinical approach is not enough. That is because depression is more than a physical response to the body's chemical imbalance. I am convinced that depression is also a spiritual issue and has a spiritual solution. When people suffering from depression attack both the clinical and spiritual issues associated with depression and anxiety, they will see better results—lasting results.

In that little hotel room in Tennessee God sowed into me the seed for this book. He beckoned me to share my story and point others toward wholeness through the power of His love and His Word. That night I felt a certain stirring in my spirit, a small voice telling me to write.

About a year before my brother died, the Spirit's voice came to me again. "Write…" As I was making dinner, "Write…" As I fell asleep, "Write…" As I folded laundry, "Write…" So I began to scribble scriptures on napkins and note my thoughts on the backs of to-do lists. As God spoke, I jotted down the thoughts He gave me. Slips of paper collected in the top drawer of my nightstand. I wasn't in a hurry. I wasn't even sure I could actually write a book. But when the Lord plants one of His seeds, it is up to Him to give us the power to accomplish the task we have been given.

In the days following my brother's death, I began to hear every day the message that had been sown in my heart four years before. "Write…" And so I did. I cannot explain how, but as I wrote, it was as if the Lord poured into me His liquid love, His heavenly words of healing to my heart. Jesus can heal anything. Nothing is too broken, too lost, or too dirty for Him to deal with. He was a carpenter; He has never been afraid to get His hands dirty. I was once a real mess. Thank goodness, Jesus didn't mind my dirt. He could see the gem beneath all the layers of mud.

In fact, healing brokenness is Jesus's specialty. He loves to gently knit us back together. Depression is awful, but my God is much bigger. I pray that this book will point you to Jesus, the great healer, and that you will find radical peace by searching the Scriptures for yourself. Ready to move toward freedom? Jesus knows the path that will get you there.

What Is Depression?

Depression is a thief. It slowly steals the soul and chips away at the very core of a person. It is cruel and convincing, making us feel as if our hearts are under the greatest of attacks. For some, depression comes after a traumatic event such as a death, a divorce, financial ruin, devastation in the form of betrayal, or abuse of the mind or body. For others it comes in waves of sadness, for no apparent reason. For some of us depression began when we simply felt overwhelmed with parts of our lives and then, before we were even aware, the waves turned into a sea that threatened to drown us. I call depression the great thief because it takes hold of a person's divine destiny and purpose, distorts the conscience, and clouds the senses. Depression is incredibly consuming. It demands all of a person's time and energy, and it cripples its victims, often leaving them listless and apathetic.

I suppose if I had to use only one term to describe this beast, I would call it the "monster of hopelessness." Depression distorts the heart so completely that the depressed person is made to think, "There is no hope." Those words are at first whispered into the soul, then shouted, until this message becomes deeply rooted into every thought, every decision, and every perception of the depressed person.

Hopelessness may start in one specific area of a person's life. For example, a person may think, "I'm lonely and depressed because I'm still single. I'll never get married, because no one wants me." This thought then works its way into multiple areas of the person's life until it begins to strangle healthy thoughts and reactions. Simply put, if these kinds of thoughts are not stopped, they will take over a person's life the way kudzu consumes a neglected garden.

My husband and I attempted our very first garden not too long ago. OK, *he* attempted to plant a garden. I helped pick the produce. As the veggies grew, we found that some creature was constantly eating away at them and ruining our beautiful harvest. It made us so mad. One day Kevin found two enormous caterpillars munching away at the tomatoes. These were not normal caterpillars; they had to have come straight out of the jungle. We even took pictures to prove to the world that we had surely discovered some new species of monster caterpillar roaming the tomato vines of Alabama. These things were as long as my hand and several inches thick. Once we found the critters a good home on the other side of our fence, our tomatoes were back to perfection. Depression can work the way those caterpillars did—it keeps eating away at a person until it is finally cast out of the garden.

Any area of our lies that lacks hope lacks the breath of God. It is the Lord who is the Creator of all pure hope, and He desires His children to live a life full of hope and joy. The devil knows that if he can steal hope from God's children, he can cripple the plans and purposes of the Father for our lives.

The claws of hopelessness tear away at the very fibers of a person's heart. The problem often begins gradually; perhaps we simply feel overwhelmed. But as it develops, our vision soon becomes clouded. Nothing seems to quite fit in our lives. It's as if no matter what we are searching for, it cannot be found. We become useless in the ministry of helping others, and selfishness begins to blossom out of nowhere. The end result is that we completely deviate from our God-given purpose and are left with a life void of hope. It is certainly not a pretty picture. But there is healing out there, and it can be found.

FINDING HEALING

Our help comes from the Lord and from Him alone. The psalmist knew this, which is why he wrote: "I lift up my eyes to the hills—where does my help come from? My help comes from the LORD, the Maker of heaven and earth" (Ps. 121:1–2).

God's desire to heal us is greater than our desire to be healed. That may seem hard for some of us to believe because we have such an incorrect view of our heavenly Father. But we must realize that men and women were never created to carry the weight of depression. That's why depression feels so impossible for us to conquer. Trying to combat it on our own is like trying to squeeze into jeans that are four sizes too small. There is no way those skinny jeans are ever going to zip up!

If we take a look at how mankind was originally created, we can get a good picture of what we were truly intended to be like. In Genesis 2 Adam and Eve walked free of sin in the garden, talking with the Lord in the cool of the day. They had no worries, no fears, no sadness, and they were in perfect relationship with the Lord. That is the true picture of how we were created to live. Anything outside that picture is not in true harmony with our intended purpose.

We were designed for a life of perfect peace and to desire to walk intimately with our God. When sin entered into the heart of humanity after Adam and Eve ate the fruit from the tree of the knowledge of good and evil, it brought with it a whole floodgate of evil waters. Suddenly things that people were never destined or created to grapple with began to take root inside of us. See, our bodies, minds, and hearts were not made to contain the darkness of depression. We were simply not designed to prosper with depression in our lives.

Recently one of my home projects was redesigning our master closet. I saw a fantastic closet makeover in a magazine, and I decided that I too wanted a lovely, well-organized, luxurious closet. The project started off as a small one, but soon I was putting in a new floor, adding trendy wallpaper, and repainting the old shelves and trim. I bought some build-it-yourself cabinets that had been advertised as "easy to put together." Halfway through building the cabinets, we realized that the inner board was missing some of the necessary holes. We ended up having to drill our own holes, which chipped the paint on the shelf.

It's kind of like that when we try to build our lives without the Lord's guidance. He created us, and He knows how we are put together. He wrote the instruction manual. When we try to build with missing instructions or try to make something fit together that doesn't quite line up, we end up with chips in our paint. Depression was never part of our owner's manual, so we need to get rid of it and rebuild with new instructions.

Thankfully, God's Word is full of instructions for us concerning how to live free of worry and fear. If you feel trapped by depression and anxiety, have had thoughts of suicide, or feel as if you are merely "existing" day to day, then I appeal to you to let God's grace begin to wash over you as you read these pages. I am not sure I can answer the "Why am I depressed?" question for you, but I can begin to answer the "How do I find healing from depression?" question.

The answer comes in two parts: ownership and abandonment. Ownership comes when we start to change the things that we can, and abandonment comes from giving to God the things that we cannot change. In other words, half the healing comes through obedience to God's Word, and the other half comes from releasing our burdens to our Father in heaven.

The path to wholeness is not an easy one. The difficulty is not necessarily in the steps you have to take to get there. Rather, anytime you invite the Lord to have His way in your life, the devil will try to remind you of your shame and disappointment and will surely stand close by to drag you back into the dark cloud of hopelessness. But as you begin this journey to healing, remember that every time you feel the spiritual tug of lost hope, you simply need to turn your face to the One who created you. Turn your face toward Jesus, the One in whom hope is found.

Oddly there is much disagreement within the church about the topic of healing. Some say that God gives us difficulties to teach us patience and endurance. Yes, the Lord does teach us through suffering, but He does not cause suffering. He does want you well, and He proved it by His death and resurrection. It is because of the sacrifice Jesus made on the cross that our hearts can be healed (Isa. 53:4–5). Let go of a spirit of religion that teaches you that you somehow deserve this pain, need it, or should endure it. Jesus came to heal, and He hasn't changed His mind about that just because His home is heaven instead of earth.

I actually once had a pastor tell me that I was suffering from depression so that when I got to heaven, I could better appreciate its goodness. I was in my early twenties when I was told this, but I was mature enough in the Lord to realize that this remark was unscriptural. If we want to be spiritually mature and able to rightly discern God's path toward healing, we must make up our minds to be radical believers of God's Word. We cannot allow the opinions of others (including well-meaning religious leaders) to cast our sails in another direction. Make up your mind today to simply believe that healing is not only a possibility for you but also a certainty.

I have heard of people who have received immediate healing from depression, just as I have heard of immediate healings from drug addiction and other disorders. I believe wholeheartedly that the Lord can and does choose to heal some in an immediate way. But it seems that the vast majority of us who have been healed from depression received healing through a process. I know, the word *process* doesn't sound like much fun.

You may ask yourself why God would choose to take you on the long road rather than an easier route. There are reasons for each of us that only the Lord may know.

One day, when we can look back over our lives, the puzzle will be a little clearer. It may not be crystal clear for you for some time, or it may never be clear in this life. Despite the *why* of it all, you must cling to the truth of God's desire for you. He says in His Word that He wants you free. I do not believe that the Lord causes or creates depression as a type of punishment or to force us into some twisted form of submission. No, the Bible teaches us the opposite.

Jesus Wants to Heal Our Souls

The Spirit of the Lord is on me, because he has anointed me to preach good news to the poor. He has sent me to proclaim *freedom for the prisoners* and recovery of sight for the blind, *to release the oppressed*, to proclaim the year of the Lord's favor.

—Luke 4:18–19, emphasis added

Jesus spoke those words from Luke as He launched into ministry. When He spoke of "freedom for the prisoners" and of His call to "release the oppressed," He was talking about providing freedom to those with bound-up hearts. His mission has not changed since He spoke those words. His message carries the same power and anointing as they did the day Jesus stood up in the synagogue and read aloud from the scroll of Isaiah. The ancient prophets foretold the Messiah's coming and wrote that He would come with healing in His wings (Mal. 4:2). Jesus fulfilled every promise the prophets proclaimed, including the one of redemption for our emotions. Take a look at what Jesus read that day in the synagogue:

He has sent me…to comfort all who mourn, and provide for those who grieve in Zion—to bestow on them
a crown of beauty instead of ashes, the oil of gladness
instead of mourning, and a garment of praise instead
of a spirit of despair. They will be called oaks of righteousness, a planting of the LORD for the display of his
splendor. They will rebuild the ancient ruins and restore
the places long devastated; they will renew the ruined
cities that have been devastated for generations.

—ISAIAH 61:1–4

I am crazy about Isaiah 61. What an amazing promise from
God given almost seven hundred years before Jesus was born.
I am certainly one of the rebuilt cities and restored fortresses
that Jesus was talking about. The great carpenter Himself
rebuilt my breached walls. Picture Jesus gently placing a crown
of beauty atop your head. Picture Him pouring the anointing
oil of gladness on you, and see the oil running down your new
garment of praise. You are the daughter of the King of kings,
and He gladly shares His glory with you.

While it's true that the Lord can use the trials of depression
to refine us, any evil done to us by others or ourselves does not
come from the hand of God. The Lord only *uses* these things
for His great purposes. My life is a beautiful example of this.
My past pain has been used to bring hope to countless others
who suffer from the kind of bondage I once endured. We live
in a fallen world, full of people with evil hearts who will selfishly crush us to get what they want. But God truly does work
all things out for His glory (Rom. 8:28).

We also have a real adversary who wants to kill us (John
10:10), and if he cannot get us through physical death, then
he will try killing off our hearts, our purposes, our minds,
our desires, our relationships, and ultimately our belief in the

Lord Jesus. Get the picture? This is a tough world. Jesus told us that it would be. But while we live in the middle of this cruel place called earth, we can walk in perfect joy, even when circumstances do not turn out as we wish or our prayers are not answered in the way we would like. The Lord bids us to drink from and wash in His fountain of joy.

So where does depression come from? We may not know *why* we get depressed, but we can know *where* this monster comes from. Depression takes place within the soul. The Bible teaches us that we are created in God's image (Gen. 1:26). When God speaks of people being created in "His image," He is speaking of us being created as triune beings, mirroring His holy and mysterious Trinity: the Father, the Son, and the Holy Spirit.

Just as God is the Father, the Son, and the Holy Spirit but only one God, so we also are three-in-one beings. We are born with a spirit and a soul, and we live in a body. The spirit and the soul are two very different parts of us, although we often confuse the two without the Word of God to teach us the difference. The Word of God can actually divide the soul and the spirit of a person (Heb. 4:12). We learn from the Bible that when we become a Christian, it is our spirit that is actually created anew. This "new creation" takes place within our spirit and then the Holy Spirit seals us, until the day when we will be with the Father forever.

Our spirit is the part of us that communicates with the Lord. God is spirit, and therefore we must speak to Him and hear Him through our spiritual eyes and ears (John 4:24). At the time of our conversion to Christ our spirit is made perfect, given the righteousness of Jesus through His blood shed on the cross. Jesus becomes our righteousness at this time, and the fullness of His spiritual gifts and callings is deposited into us all at once. It is as if He downloads the very DNA of Jesus into us and makes us fully part of God's family. It can take us a lifetime to realize all the power that is stored within our spirits through Jesus.

As we learn to die to our selfish nature, the spirit person inside us is made stronger. Sadly, however, most believers never learn to function in the fullness of spirit, which the Lord intends to be the source of our ministry to others. Most believers operate much more from the soul than the spirit and therefore quench the possibilities laid up inside us through Jesus.

Our soul is made up of our mind, will, and emotions, and this is also the part of us that houses our sinful nature. Think about what goes through your mind, what your will tends to desire, and how you operate in your emotions. You should quickly figure out that this is the part of us that the devil can attack. The enemy attacks this part of us because he can gain access to it, just as he can gain access to our bodies. The only thing he does not have legal access to, once we are made new by the Lord Jesus, is our spirit.

Depression and anxiety, along with a multitude of other debilitating conditions, are all-out attacks on the soul. The devil relentlessly attacks the thoughts that go through our minds, tries to convince us to exercise our wills and reject the Lord's plan, and certainly assaults our emotions. Depression is a war against our hope, and anxiety is a war against our peace. It is helpful for us to know where the battle lines are drawn so that we know how to plan our counterattack. Your journey toward healing is essentially a war campaign that will target these two battlegrounds of depression and anxiety that take place within our souls. With each step you take, you will regain ground that the enemy has stolen or corrupted.

Our spirits are made perfect upon salvation, but our souls can remain in rebellion, sin, selfishness, and pride. Obviously our souls are not made perfect upon salvation. And I am sure you would agree that our bodies are not made perfect upon salvation either. It is within our souls and in our bodies that Satan fights us. Our souls and our bodies are the battlefields, and we can surrender to the enemy or wage war against him. It's our choice, and every day we decide who will take more ground within this fight: the devil or us.

So we now know that depression is a battle within the soul, but what effect does this have on the body? It is well documented that depressed people often see negative changes within their bodies as well as in their thoughts and feelings. These can include fatigue, pain, a weakened immune system, and many other signals that something isn't right. When we are depressed, the chemicals in our bodies produce either too much or not enough of what we need so we encounter attacks on multiple fronts. A health care provider will most likely deal with the physical effects and causes of depression, but we also need to treat its spiritual effects and causes. It is my hope that as you find healing in your soul, you will see the physical effects of depression decline as well.

We Need God to Fight for Us

So what does the Lord say about overcoming the difficulties in these troubled souls of ours? When we are depressed, it can seem at times as if our own spirits are attacking us, waging war against the good things of God within us. And this analogy of a war is somewhat accurate. This "flesh" of ours, as the Bible calls it, is in rebellion against the very Person of God Himself. The solution to gaining victory over our selfish soul, our flesh, is to die to it. Paul said it this way: "Those who belong to Christ Jesus have crucified the sinful nature with its passions and desires" (Gal. 5:24).

This way of dealing with our souls may seem rather harsh, considering these are our thoughts and emotions. Didn't God give us these aspects of ourselves? How can our emotions become so negative? So out of control? Why are our spirits made perfect upon salvation while our souls remain so messed up?

It is because our souls and our bodies, as long as we live on this earth, are subject to attack by Satan. Even worse, we ourselves can attack our own souls and bodies by our careless decisions. We can gorge on junk food and hurt our bodies, and we can gorge on the things of this world and hurt our souls. Other people can hurt these two parts of us as well. Because we can be attacked from various directions, many of us walk around with open wounds on our bodies and scars in our souls, and we have no clue as to how we can be healed. As a result, we spend a lot of money and time bandaging up and hiding all the wounds deep within us.

Only the Lord Jesus can come in and heal our broken hearts and restore the things that have been stolen. Surely you have tried very hard to be relieved of this weight called depression but, perhaps, have had little success. Maybe the fact that you are reading this book is a way of admitting that you can't fix this problem yourself, that it has gone too far. Each of us needs Jesus's power and wisdom in order to take a step in a new direction. His power provides us with the help we cannot give ourselves, and His wisdom shows us how to walk in freedom, prevent further self-damage, and then stay free.

Do not be surprised if things get harder before they get better. The devil will certainly fight to keep you locked up in the prison of depression, fear, and anxiety. Know that the

Lord has greater power than the devil does and that in God's Spirit there is rest. This battle has already been decided. *And the Lord wins every time.* The freedom God gives *is free*, but it will cost you a great deal. It will cost your time, your patience, and most of all, your obedience to do and release what the Lord tells you to. God takes our acts of faith and mixes them with His supernatural power to bring about His perfect will.

Of course, the Lord can only fight for those of us who are His children. God has given each of us a free will so we may come to Him of our own choice. He will not force His will or His goodness on us. He will only move when we invite Him to do so.

I often tell the students who attend the Bible study I teach that the Lord is moved by our faith, not by our need. If He responded to need alone, no one would go hungry or be sick or live without basic human dignities. And that is not the reality we see around us. You see, faith is the currency in the kingdom of God. Faith is a substance, and it can be measured by the Father. The wonderful news is that we don't need much of it in order to move mountains (Matt. 17:20). We just need enough for God to work with. One drop of faith in the Father's hand can accomplish miracles.

Are you a man or woman of faith? Have you made Jesus Lord in your life? Do you believe that the Bible is true and that Jesus is the key to your becoming a child of God? Only when you can answer yes to these questions can you become one of God's children. Those are not my words but the Lord's. If you are pausing here and realizing that you do not believe in God the Creator, in Jesus the only Son, and in the Holy Spirit the Teacher, then I have to say this book will not be very useful to you.

Without God's hand guiding you through healing and

without His sweet presence in your life, I don't have a clue how to help you. All I can do is point you toward God's path of healing—the path that begins in Him and also leads to Him. God requires us to have faith in Jesus if we want to one day be with Him and to experience His presence here on earth. If you would like to know Jesus as Lord, please pray the prayer below and mean it with all your heart. Once you have asked Him into your heart, you are His, and that makes you a candidate for a miracle.

> *Dear Lord, I come to You right now, and I lay my life at Your altar. I come with faith that You are the one true, living God and that Your Son Jesus lived, died, and rose again to provide eternal life for me. I lay aside my desires, and I ask that You fill me instead with Your desires. Fill me with Your Holy Spirit. Use my life for Your glory. I now choose to follow You, and I believe that You will lead me. Teach me how to love others as You love me. Reveal Jesus to me as I study Your holy Word. I love You, and I will forever serve You as Your child. Thank You for making me new, for making me alive in Christ, and for writing my name in the Lamb's book of life in heaven. Thank You for calling me into the family of God! In Jesus's name, amen!*

It may seem difficult or even impossible to hand over control of our lives to someone else, but it is actually far more difficult for us to hold on to our own will and our human attempts to be healed than it is to trust the Lord. God doesn't need much from us—just our everything. As we learn to give up our own efforts to be healed and let the Lord take over as ruler of our lives, we will stumble into a place of deep and meaningful rest.

God's Love Letter to You

As you move down the path toward healing, I cannot promise that troubles will not come or that you will not slip and fall along the way. The Lord, however, does make promises in His Word, and He makes them *to you*. In His promises lies the fullness of peace and hope. In His arms you can find rest for your weary mind.

One of the most precious and beautiful truths we can see in God's Word is that the Lord understands what we go through. He is not naïve, too holy to deal with our messes, or unavailable to meet us where we are. He is OK with us when we are raw and hurting. He is OK with us even when we show anger toward Him or accuse Him of somehow allowing our disappointments.

The Bible is full of accounts of believers who went through awful, tragic events and heartache and yet also felt free to vocalize their heartache to the Lord. It is not our emotions or perceptions that make us acceptable to God but our belief in Jesus and what He accomplished on the cross. The Lord gave us the stories about these men and women of God and their heartaches so that we could see through them that our Father does understand our hearts' cry. He not only hears our cries for help, but He also responds to us with love and grace. He knows exactly what we are going through—every thought, every emotion, every pain. Not one tear goes unnoticed. Not convinced? Let's look at Scripture and see if what we find there echoes any of your emotions.

The Book of Psalms is full of human feeling. Many of the other books of the Bible are filled with dates and times, or the genealogies of certain families, but the Book of Psalms is truly chapter after chapter of how the psalmist actually *felt*. In this book we get a glimpse into the thoughts of a man named David and into the very mind and heart of God.

David is famous for many great feats of courage but also for his great sin of adultery with a woman named Bathsheba. After David sinned with Bathsheba, she became pregnant, so he had her husband killed. Thank goodness, David wrote about all his feelings, both good and bad, so we can see that we are not alone. His words, recorded thousands of years before Jesus came, remind us of how all of humanity shares this longing for peace in our innermost parts.

Through David's circumstances we get a sense of God's great love for David—and for us. Those of you who suffer depression will recognize the cry of a man who at times was under great persecution within his soul. See if you can identify with any of his words:

> How long must I wrestle with my thoughts and every day have sorrow in my heart?
> —PSALM 13:2

> The cords of death entangled me; the torrents of destruction overwhelmed me.
> —PSALM 18:4

> My God, my God, why have you forsaken me? Why are you so far from saving me, so far from the words of my groaning?
> —PSALM 22:1

> Be merciful to me, O LORD, for I am in distress; my eyes grow weak with sorrow, my soul and my body with grief. My life is consumed by anguish and my years by

groaning; my strength fails because of my affliction, and my bones grow weak. Because of all my enemies, I am the utter contempt of my neighbors; I am a dread to my friends—those who see me on the street flee from me. I am forgotten by them as though I were dead; I have become like broken pottery.

—Psalm 31:9–12

"I have become like broken pottery." I remember feeling that way. In fact, I believe that depression is no better articulated and described than within the very words of the Bible. The Scriptures perfectly capture a picture of those who are depressed, those "consumed by anguish."

As you stand at the beginning of the road to healing and wholeness, know that a loving God understands your pain and has left you His love letter, the Bible, to encourage and strengthen you. In it He gives you a blueprint for finding peace within your soul. Although the Lord does not promise a perfect world around you, He can bring you to a place of rest and healing despite any storm in your life. He did not create your depression, but because of His love for you, He is standing by to lift you out of it.

Dig Deeper

1. Do any of the scriptures from the Book of Psalms talk about feelings that are familiar to you? If so, which ones?

2. Do you think the Lord understands what you are going through? Why or why not?

3. In what way is your soul under attack?

Assignments

Read Isaiah 61. Write your favorite verse from this passage.

Exercise 1: Take stock of your mind, will, and emotions.

Confronting the state of your soul will require fearlessness on your part. "Taking stock" can take many forms so long as you remain true to the heart of this exercise. Take inventory of your soul. Look at what is really there as well as what's missing, then record these things so you can examine them. As you write, use descriptive words for how you feel. This helps you release your pain and give it a voice. Something very powerful takes place when we become aware of our negative attitudes, thoughts, and desires.

This exercise can be done through freestyle writing (writing whatever thoughts come to your mind), making a list of your feelings, or using any other form of self-expression that will capture where you are right now.

This may take you some time to figure out, maybe even a few days. We rarely force ourselves to be totally honest about where we are mentally, emotionally, and otherwise. We spend much of our time covering up or pretending that we are OK, when that is the furthest thing from the truth. This exercise will allow you to see what is going on in your soul without your having to cover anything up. The more time you put into this inventory, the greater the benefits will be for you when it is complete.

As you prepare to take stock of your mind, will, and emotions, ask yourself what is healthy and unhealthy in each of the following areas:

- Your mind
- Your will
- Your emotions

Exercise 2: Create a vision for your soul.

"Where there is no *vision*, the people perish" (Prov. 29:18, KJV, emphasis added). What is your vision? Once you have taken stock of your soul, make a list of how you want each area of your soul to look. What do you wish was different? What do you wish you did more of? What seems to be missing from your soul inventory? Allow yourself to create a concrete vision of how you want your mind, will, and emotions to operate.

Prayer time

Now that you have taken stock of your soul and created a vision of what it *could* become, spend some time praying over your two lists. Block off a time when you won't have any distractions. I suggest playing quiet praise music in the background to allow your spirit to begin to worship and enter into God's presence. Be very specific in your prayers. Pray over each area that is unhealthy, and ask Jesus to heal you from the inside out. Take as long as you need for this; don't rush this precious time with Jesus. After you pray, write down three things that the Lord showed you during this exercise.

> *Holy Spirit, please come in and touch my soul. Fill my heart, my mind, and my emotions with Your Spirit. Wash away all the things in my heart, mind, and emotions that are not pleasing to You. Fill my heart with love for You. Fill my mind with healthy and holy thoughts. Teach me how to be submitted to You in my emotions. Lord, give me new vision for my life and a new attitude within my heart. Reveal to me Your love for me. In Jesus's name, amen.*

Chapter 2

CONFRONTING PRIDE

The LORD sustains the humble.
—*Psalm 147:6*

O NE OF MY closest friends is wrought with pride. We have known each other for over ten years, and she has never once admitted that she has done anything wrong. In fact, even when caught in a naughty act, she remains resolute in her innocence. She thinks she is superior to others, and because of her snobby attitude, I am one of her only friends. She spends an insane amount of time making sure she looks good. She is cute, but if you were to ask her about her looks, she would say that she is more beautiful than any runway model. OK, before you start thinking badly of me, I have to tell you that I am describing my calico cat, Sweetpea. And yes, Sweetpea is a very prideful kitty.

Some pride is clearly evident, as in Sweetpea's case, but most of our pride issues are much more subtle. It takes God's flashlight shining on these areas in order for us to see them.

You may be asking why in the world I would include a lesson on pride in a book about depression and anxiety. I asked the question too when I first started discussing this book with a ministry girlfriend of mine. She, like me, had been healed from depression and anxiety, and as we sat on the couch in my basement discussing topics I wanted to cover, she suggested that I add the topic of pride. Her suggestion seemed silly to me, because I didn't think of pride as part of the DNA of a depressed person. Depressed people don't often think highly of themselves, do they? Pride certainly was not at the root of depression—or was it? As I began to seek the Lord about this issue of pride, He showed me that without a doubt pride was and is a very important area of weakness in the life of someone who is depressed.

What Pride Looks Like

The real recipe for pride is self-centeredness with a touch of jealousy. And as harsh as this may sound, most depressed people are full of pride—but they are masters at masking it under insecurities, fears, and negative self-talk. Often when someone going through depression talks about his issues, he will repeatedly say, "You just don't understand..." These words are the result of a defensive attitude, and this motto becomes part of his very identity.

"No one understands..." It is as if when we use these words we feel the need to prove to anyone who will listen that we suffer more than others and that this makes us special. It is more than simply sharing our struggles—it is a way of mustering up attention and sympathy. And the answer is yes—it's true that no one understands the burdens we carry. Only the Lord Jesus understands.

It is not right for us to become frustrated with others if they are not convinced of how awful our lives are or if they do not become depressed alongside us. One of the most frustrating things I remember about my years in depression was the jealousy I had toward the people around me who were actually enjoying life. It really quite disgusted me. Here I was, full of pain, hurting every day, and they got to walk around with big smiles. I was somehow numb, watching everyone else live while I walked around in a fog. I was annoyed by others' good news, promotions, or funny stories, and I was sure that they even laughed a little more than usual when they were around me to rub things in. My behavior sounds foolish to me now. But at one time it prohibited me from having rich, full, two-way relationships. I'm sure I was difficult to be around at times, and I shudder now to think about my attitude during that time.

I shared my dorm room during a portion of my college years with a naturally happy, joyful friend. She would be smiling as soon as she got up every morning, and it really grated on my nerves. (I am so embarrassed to admit that now!) She was up every morning by six o'clock, reading her Bible, while I lay ten feet away from her in bed, desperate to keep sleeping until I had to get up for class.

I was a big mess at this point, and I had no idea how to find a way out. I was miserable, and my roommate wasn't—and the more she laughed, the more I felt my misery. Life just seemed easier for her than it was for me, full of fun and open doors. Now I realize that I could have been just as happy, just as care-free as she was in that little dorm room. I can see it so clearly now that I am on the other side of depression.

I am now one of those happy people who really love life. But I see this jealous attitude in others who suffer from depression, so I extend compassion to them in this area since I once walked in their shoes. But many people are not able to extend that amount of compassion, and they ultimately walk away from a relationship with a depressed person. If you have lost relationships through your struggle with depression, it could be because your despondency became too much for the other person to handle.

Not every depressed or anxious person easily verbalizes

their struggle to others, but many do, and their constant negativity will wreak havoc on their relationships. Anytime we look to another person to fulfill our needs, listen to us unload our emotions, or provide healing, we will be searching for something from the relationship that the other person is not able to give us. Others cannot carry us through life. I spent a lot of time looking to others to fix my heart, with little to no result. If you are where I was, it is time to stop being needy with people and to begin needing and seeking a relationship with Jesus.

People will disappoint, but Jesus never will. However, rather than pouring out their burdens on other people, a great many depressed people suffer in silence. It's not because they cannot afford professional help or find support. They suffer in silence because exposing their "weakness" to the world would mean that everyone would know they are not perfect. Many won't ask for help until their depression has progressed to a point at which something has to break—or until it is too late altogether.

Pride is kind of like cancer. If we go to the doctor when a lump is small, the cancer's progression can usually be halted, and our prognosis is pretty good. But if we wait until that lump becomes massive and has grown to stage four cancer, much more damage is done, and healing becomes more difficult. Don't hesitate to invite the Lord to do His healing work, and don't hold back from seeking peace.

Admitting that we need help—and that we aren't managing our internal health very well on our own—takes a great deal of courage. Even more importantly, though, it requires laying down that nasty little thing called pride. It is OK if some of our friends and family know about our struggles. We need people around us who can minister to us. They are more likely to do that if they know what we are going through. We need to give people a chance. If the ones we turn to do not show compassion, then we can turn our attention elsewhere, but for goodness' sake, we must let someone know what we are really going through!

Another ingredient in pride, and one that is particularly dangerous, is self-protection. Often the devil takes something that the Lord has created for our benefit, such as the desire to keep ourselves safe, and he twists it until not only is the benefit squeezed out, but it also becomes dangerous and evil. The devil cannot create anything; only the Lord has creative powers. Satan can only take these God-created things and contaminate them.

Our loving Father put the tendency for self-protection within us. For example, if someone raises a hand to hit us, it is natural for us to react by positioning our limbs to block our bodies or by running away. This kind of response is innate, and it is good. But Satan takes our God-given desire to protect ourselves and convinces us that if we do not take action *every* time we might get hurt emotionally, we will suffer great consequences.

The devil even goes so far as to convince believers that if we don't take matters into our own hands, surely God won't come through for us. So instead of letting God protect us, we spend a lot of time trying to keep ourselves safe. People who have been deeply hurt are particularly prone to say, "I can and will protect myself emotionally." What they are really saying, even if they don't know it, is that they want to control the outcome of potentially painful circumstances. They do not trust God. And that attitude reeks of pride.

The opposite of pride is humility. There is something magnetic about people who possess a truly humble spirit. Other people are drawn to this kind of attitude, and God is too. I suppose if anyone in the Bible had a reason to become prideful, it would have been Moses. Let's take a look at his outstanding résumé:

- He is one of the best-selling authors of all time (he wrote the first five books of the Old Testament).

- He was raised in Pharaoh's palace and educated by the most brilliant minds of his day.

- He met with God many times, and God revealed to Moses great mysteries of the faith.

- He was a leader of millions of people—the chosen people of God.

- He walked with great authority on the earth. Under his command God worked awesome miracles that people still talk about today.

That is a pretty impressive rundown. Moses actually got to see the glory of God. He could have bragged about this encounter to his church buddies, but because of his great wisdom, he retained a humble heart. Here is what God had to say about Moses: "Now Moses was a very humble man, more humble than anyone else on the face of the earth" (Num. 12:3). I would call that quite a compliment. It seems that as Moses grew in the Lord, he also grew in humility.

Want people at work to like you? Become a humble, authentic person. Want your family dynamics to change? Make sure there is no chip on your shoulder.

THINGS PRIDE MAKES US DO

Pride builds such high walls around our souls that it blocks out even the Lord. It is as if *we* want to take responsibility for the outcomes of circumstances in our life. But when we focus on taking care of outcomes, we spend less energy taking responsibility for our actions. That is backward. We should be taking full responsibility for our actions and leaving the outcomes to the Lord.

I sometimes hear Christians use tired clichés to blame others for their actions. "The devil made me do it," they'll say, or, "I did it because of my terrible childhood," or, "I acted this way because of what that person did to me." We in the Western world particularly have become experts at making excuses to avoid taking responsibility. These excuses are often heavily connected with our past in some way. While our past does shape us, once we come to know the Lord Jesus, *all* things are put under His blood. God does not want our past to inhibit our today or cause us to worry about tomorrow.

Depressed and anxious people also often become controllers. Because their internal emotions are out of control, they tend to focus on controlling external factors. Some resort to manipulation. Many depressed women I have counseled use their emotions to manipulate others, especially their families. Because their manipulation is masked by their tears, it is often misjudged for true distress. "If you don't do this, I am going to hurt myself..." "You don't love me if you..." "I need your attention *right away* because..." We should never use demands or threats of self-harm to get our way.

If you are thinking of hurting yourself, seek immediate professional help. But know that it is never right to use those types of words to try and make others submit to your will.

Emotional manipulation may get you what you want in the short term, but over time it will exhaust your loved ones and cause them to walk away from you. Emotional manipulation may cause others to give in to you, but it will never bring you the love you are looking for.

Trying to control the outcomes of situations in our lives also leads us to make excuses for our behavior. Excuses may be a hallmark of modern Western civilization, but some of the followers of Jesus were pretty good at it too. In Luke 14 we see some of Jesus's disciples giving excuses for why they could not follow Him. One said he had to wait until his father died, and another said he needed to take care of a piece of land he had just purchased. Little did these men know that they would be missing out on walking the earth with their very Creator. What an honor to be invited to travel with Jesus—to be invited by God to hang out. But because of their excuses, they didn't obey Jesus, and ultimately they lost out on witnessing the greatest mysteries and miracles in all eternity.

Pride, in addition to these other negative behaviors, makes us choose our own path instead of God's. We think we can do things better. We think we know what we need. "It's my life, and surely taking things into my own hands won't be that big a deal, right?" But decisions made from pride will always cause us to miss out on God's full blessings. Pride is sin, no matter how we dress it up.

When my husband and I bought our house six years ago, we knew it would take a few years for us to fix it up the way we really wanted it. The master bath had a truly awful brown-beige tile in the shower along with a swirl-patterned sink top to match. The previous owner had painted the cabinets white and changed the color on the walls in an attempt to de-uglify that bathroom. He had even bought accessories in that same awful brown-beige in order to make everything "blend."

Since like him we couldn't yet afford to remodel the bathroom, we brought in a decorator to help us decide how best to arrange things. We talked about lighting, and we chose accessories that would work with the existing color palette. The decorator encouraged us to replace several items, such as the mirrors. At the end of the day, however, we realized that we could paint that bathroom any color of the rainbow, but until that tile and sink top hit the Dumpster, it was always going to be an ugly master bath. Let me tell you, it felt wonderful the day we ripped out every single ugly tile and replaced the vanity. It was like we had moved into a new house!

Pride can be like those ugly tiles. We can decorate around it and try to make it tolerable, but we can never cover it up. Once the pride is removed, however, a beautiful new space is created within us that we didn't even realize could possibly exist.

We Need God, and We Need Others

"In his pride the wicked does not seek him; in all his thoughts *there is no room for God*" (Ps. 10:4, emphasis added). Pride actually keeps us from seeking the Lord. Satan whispers in our ears, "You can handle this depression on your own. You don't need other people, and you don't need God." This lie is especially easy for us to believe when we have been deeply hurt by people we love. We begin to believe that no one can be trusted, not even our heavenly Father.

But that is far from the truth. We do need people. Our heavenly Father designed us that way. He meant for us to have great relationships, both with Him and with other people, so that we have someone with us when we go through the rough days of life. "If one falls down, his friend can help him up. But pity the man who falls and has no one to help him up!" (Eccles. 4:10). If we don't have friends or family to help us up, the Lord says He has pity for us. It is important for us, particularly when we are depressed, to seek out healthy, God-filled relationships—and to give up some friends who don't meet that description. Depression loves to isolate us, and isolation, as we will discuss later, can lead to pride.

Psalm 147:6 says, "The LORD sustains the humble but casts the wicked to the ground." I don't know about you, but I need sustaining. It is with a humble heart that we are to seek relationship with the Lord and to approach our relationships with others.

Sometimes people wrongly think that being humble means living in insecurity or welcoming abuse, but this is far from the biblical description. A humble spirit is one without a hint of pride. It's what is left after we allow the Lord to show us our pride and remove it from our souls. To be humble is to take on the heart of Jesus. Humility is the subtlest but most incredibly powerful action we can use against the devil and against depression. Being humble makes room for the Holy Spirit and releases God's healing power into your life. An added bonus to cultivating a humble heart is that everyone around us will benefit from our new perspective. Believe me, people will notice the change in us when we drop our pride and take on humility.

Often depressed people, in their refusal to get help from the Lord or from those who love them, turn to self-medicating. I have seen this in the lives of my family members, who used drugs and alcohol. Self-medicating takes on many forms: binge eating, alcohol, drugs, prescription pills, sexual acts outside of marriage, extreme shopping, gambling, self-cutting, and many other destructive behaviors. These behaviors are all rooted in pride, whether we realize it or not. Anytime we look to false comforts to fix us instead of God, we are saying to the Lord, "I don't need Your help. This pill will do the trick." When we turn to negative behaviors instead of God, it grieves the Lord greatly. He wants to be the One we run to with our pain.

"Though the LORD is on high, he looks upon the lowly, but the proud he knows from afar" (Ps. 138:6). The Lord desires to touch us and heal us, but sometimes we will not let Him. Pride tells us to hold on to our problems. Pride tells us not to admit that we need help in a big way. Pride tells us not to seek out someone whom we can trust to help us. But it's time to try a new approach. Your way may not be working. *If you truly want to be set free, fully give yourself over to the process of God's healing.*

Admit to the Lord, first of all, that you need His help. Then, after you have acknowledged your need to the Lord, ask another believer to stand with you in prayer throughout this process of healing. *You have nothing to lose but your depression.*

There are only two rules to apply in choosing your special prayer partner: first, choose someone who is a growing Christian believer, and second, choose someone whom you trust—a friend, a family member, your spouse, or someone from your church. Before jumping to a decision, though, seek the Lord about whom you should approach. You may be surprised at the people the Lord tells you to talk with. Only the Holy Spirit knows who will be the best fit for this assignment.

This prayer partner will now become part of your healing process over the coming weeks. It takes a humble heart to ask for help, but reaching out will result in great blessing for you. Someone other than you needs to know what is really going on inside your heart. Some of the people in your life may already know that you are suffering with depression, but having a specific prayer partner who knows your secrets and who will not judge you is especially important.

I encourage you to share everything you comfortably can with your prayer partner and to keep in regular contact with him or her as you walk through this journey. Releasing any pride you have will usher in a humble heart, and a humble heart invites healing. Asking the Lord, a prayer partner, or a good Christian counselor for help is a wonderful step toward wholeness. Cut the noose of pride from your life, and you will certainly begin to walk in a greater level of freedom from depression.

So long, pride!

Dig Deeper

1. Do you have any unhealthy relationships in your life right now? If so, list them.

2. What false comforts might you be using to mask your pain?

3. Are you ready to remove your false comforts? If so, how will you do this?

4. Do you have, or have you ever had, jealousy toward a cheerful, satisfied person? If so, what did that person have that you wanted?

5. What does it mean to have a humble heart?

Assignments

Exercise 1: Seek out a prayer partner (or partners) and ask for help.

Contact the person whom you would like to be your prayer partner, and ask that person if he or she would be willing to pray with you through this season of your life. You may even decide to choose more than one person—it is up to you. When you have established your prayer partner, share with that person what you are going through. Be fearless in truly sharing your heart's cry. You may want to let your partner know about this book and that you will be doing some special assignments as you work through the study. Ask your prayer partner to pray every day for you as you seek healing. Ask him to be available to you to throughout the study to discuss the things the Lord is speaking to you and to keep you accountable to the principles you are learning.

The key to getting the most value from this exercise is to not hold back. Make a promise to this person that if you ever feel suicidal or think about engaging in other self-destructive behavior, you will call immediately. The Lord often brings people into our lives to walk with us in faith. Allow the Lord to begin to use others to hold your hand.

Write down the name(s) of your chosen prayer partner(s).

Exercise 2: Confront any area of pride in your life.

Start by taking stock of any areas in your life in which pride exists. Ask the Lord to reveal these areas to you, and as He speaks to you, make a list. Then ask the Lord to remove the pride within your heart. Spend time praying over the specific areas you have written down, and ask the Holy Spirit to wash you clean as you confess your sin. Acknowledge your complete dependence on the Lord to heal you. Ask the Lord to put within you a humble heart.

Prayer time

This step on the journey to healing may push you out of your comfort zone, but hang in there with me. Now is the time to for you to admit to yourself and to God, your loving Father, that you cannot in any way dig yourself out of the pit of depression. Spend some time in prayer now, and acknowledge that only the Lord's power can save you from living in depression. Acknowledge that only He can restore you to wholeness. Only He has the power to transform your life. Release to God all your "trying," and tell Him how much you need His love and grace in order to reach freedom.

> *Lord, I acknowledge that You alone have the power of healing. I cannot save myself from the power of depression, and I ask that You send me miraculous power from on high so that I can reach a place of total restoration. Father, I release to You all the false comforts that I have put ahead of You. Forgive me, and send Your Holy Spirit to comfort me instead. Write Your healing words upon my heart.*

Chapter 3

REINTRODUCE HOPE

May the God of hope fill you with all joy and peace
as you trust in him, so that you may overflow
with hope by the power of the Holy Spirit.

—*Romans 15:13*

ON'T YOU JUST hate losing things? I do. We all lose our car keys, and I don't know how many times I have misplaced my sunglasses or TV remote.

I especially hate losing things I am really fond of. Before I met my husband, I traveled to Italy with a girlfriend of mine to sightsee and to enjoy the country's fabulous architecture and food. Back then I was really into packing light (now I pack way too much), so I brought only two pairs of shoes. One was my all-time favorite pair of black shoes. I know, I surely committed some kind of female misdemeanor by packing only two pairs of shoes, but what can I say? I was young and foolish.

My favorite black shoes went with everything in my wardrobe and also happened to be the most comfortable shoes in my closet. I adored those shoes. But unfortunately I left them under a chair in one of our Italian hotels and never saw them again. I was stuck with only one pair of shoes for the rest of the trip, and I was so mad that I had lost my perfect shoes. Years later I am still irritated with myself about it.

There are things in life that we don't mind losing all that

much, such as a sock now and again in the laundry or an item we would shove into a junk drawer. I am a master at losing receipts, which is OK until I need to take something back. Just as we can lose tangible items, we can also lose things in the spiritual realm. Hope is one of those things that is often lost— and I know, because I have misplaced mine before.

Where Did You Put Your Hope?

Hope is one of those qualities that we may not pay a whole lot of attention to until it is gone. And once it has gone missing in a certain area of life, it can be a little difficult to find again. A loss of hope is one of the main markers of depression. But when we reintroduce hope into our lives, our depression will decrease. Hopelessness is a weary land to slog through, and it takes faith to walk out of it.

It can be hard to bring something back into our lives if we feel as if it walked out on us. Maybe that is how your hope left. You wanted it to stay, but one day it walked out the front door of your heart and hasn't returned. Or maybe you kicked it out. One too many disappointments came your way, and you'd had enough. To protect yourself you figured it would be easier to tell that hope to hit the road. You were not going to wait around to be disappointed again. However you lost your hope, the fact is that your old friend hope is no longer in every room of your heart, and it has left behind a hole that you have been unable to fill.

I understand. I have had hope walk out on me, and I have kicked it out too, but in either case I was left feeling miserable. If you have fallen into discouragement and sadness, you need to be reintroduced to hope. Actually, I should use the word *introduce*, because for some of you it has been so long since you've seen hope that you might have forgotten what it looks like.

You may be thinking that you want to skip over this chapter, since having hope didn't get you anywhere before. Why try again? You may be thinking, "Jenny, I used to have hope, but if you only knew how many disappointments I've experienced, you wouldn't ask me to start hoping again." And if I thought hope was based only on maintaining positive circumstances in life, then I would agree with you. But if our hope is based only on our past successes or failures, then it would be something that could come and go like the tide. If I were to tell you that hope could live eternally within you regardless of your circumstances, would you be interested in making a place for it again? Keep reading, and maybe you will become convinced.

"Where then is my hope? Who can see any hope for me?" (Job 17:15). We need to ask the same question Job did: Where did all our hope go? A verse in Proverbs may give us the key: "*Hope deferred makes the heart sick*, but a longing fulfilled is a tree of life" (Prov. 13:12, emphasis added). It is the disappointments in life—those things that we wanted to happen a certain way but didn't—that steal our hope. Maybe something did not happen in our timeline, or we prayed about a need but never received an answer. "Surely God could have answered those prayers," we tell ourselves. Usually it's after a string of disappointments in several areas of our lives that we begin to give up. But ultimately we have to reach the point at which we accept that there will be many things in life that we won't understand until we get to heaven.

Life is full of disappointments, isn't it? Some disappointments are small, such as when we really don't like how a haircut turned out or we have to work again on the weekend. Bigger disappointments could be the loss of a child, another miscarriage, failing to get the promotion we have waited two years for, a spouse walking out, a business failing, or having to postpone retirement—again. Disappointments can seem overwhelming at times. I have had my fair share—not getting into medical school, watching a business not take off as planned, losing my brother way too early, and on and on. Any one of us could write a sad country song about our troubles.

What Hope Is and Is Not

"My God, my God, why have you forsaken me?" Jesus cried from the cross (Matt. 27:46). Jesus understands how we feel. Even He, the Son of God, asked "Why?" of His Father during a dark hour in His own life. I have had way too many "God, why?" moments in my life. I bet you have too. We ask why when we cannot see the purpose in our pain. Often, though, I don't get an answer to the question—at least not right away. When my brother died, I was desperately looking for the purpose in his death. How could the Lord make something beautiful out of such a desperately tragic event?

I began to find peace only when I started writing. The Lord began to speak to me in sweet whispers and to tell me lovingly that in His hands all things could be made lovely—even the events that seem to be born out of dark places. After walking through the blackness of depression and finding the light of Jesus, I can now see purpose in my pain. I can share my story of redemption over and over to make a way of hope for others who are hurting.

As hard as it is for us to let go of our need to know why things have happened, we certainly find freedom when we do. We must make it to the place at which we can boldly say, "Lord, even if I do not know the reason, I still choose to love and follow You. My love for You is not dependent on my perception of what You *have* or *have not* done for me." Let me tell you, it can be quite the journey to get to that place! It might mean long nights in tearful prayer, or it might mean daily letting go of *having* to know the answer to the question "Why, God?" Whatever you need to do to get there, do it. Don't stop until those words of acceptance and trust can flow from you without any hesitation. If you cannot say your love for God is not dependent on your perception of what He has or has not done for you, then really your love for God has strings attached.

Ouch. I know that hurt.

If our love for the Father is dependent upon what He has done for us or given to us, then something is wrong. The one act of dying on the cross to achieve our salvation should be enough for Jesus to garner our love for eternity. No strings attached. Real hope in the Lord means giving Him the glory, no matter what. It means *choosing* to hope in Him, no matter how long our list of troubles seems to be.

Now *hope* is one of those words that our Western language and lifestyle have completely cheapened. "Hope you have a nice day." We hear that every time we go through a checkout line or order food at a drive-through window. "I hope it doesn't rain today." "I hope the store has that sweater in my size." We throw the word *hope* around all the time and don't even think about what we are saying. We use it as a way of saying what we wish will happen. This usage is actually quite different from the way the word *hope* is used in the Bible. I found the following definition in a Bible dictionary:

> Biblical hope is the anticipation of a favorable outcome under God's guidance. More specifically, hope is the confidence that what God has done for us in the past guarantees our participation in what God will do in the

future. This contrasts to the world's definition of hope as "a feeling that what is wanted will happen." Understood in this way, hope can denote either a baseless optimism or a vague yearning after an unattainable good. If hope is to be genuine hope, however, it must be founded on something (or someone) which affords reasonable grounds for confidence in its fulfillment. The Bible bases its hope in God and His saving acts.[1]

I like the phrase "baseless optimism," because it describes so well how most of us approach the concept of hope. Unlike the popular version of hope, which is based upon our perception of circumstances, biblical hope is wrapped up and discovered in the person of Jesus. It is not merely a feeling but a tangible substance we can obtain only through the Lord. "And hope does not disappoint us, because God has poured out his love into our hearts by the Holy Spirit, whom he has given us" (Rom. 5:5).

"The eyes of the LORD are on those who fear him, on those whose hope is in his unfailing love" (Ps. 33:18). Our hope is in Him, through Him, because of Him. If your hope has been wrapped up in a relationship, in your career, in your future, in finding a spouse, in finding success, or in anything the world offers, then your hope anchor has been dropped into the wrong ocean. It is settling to know that "we have this *hope* as an *anchor* for the soul, firm and secure. It enters the inner sanctuary behind the curtain, where Jesus, who went before us, has entered on our behalf" (Heb. 6:19–20, emphasis added).

SPENDING TIME WITH GOD

In the Old Testament tabernacle there was an inner sanctuary, the special place that God the Father had chosen as His throne room here on earth. It represented His presence among the

Hebrew people. Through the work of Jesus on the cross, we now have access to that sanctuary's counterpart in heaven. We are welcome to go behind the curtain, into the presence of God. It is as if Jesus has invited us into His family room to come and hang out with Him and His dad. We get to eat spaghetti dinner with Him, and He tells us stories, and we laugh together.

As God's children, we get an invitation every day from the Father to come and join Him in His inner room. This inner-room invitation gives us full access to all the blessings and gifts the Lord has reserved for His children. Hope is one of these precious, precious gifts. If our anchor is firmly embedded in the streams of the river of life, then hope will do its work in our hearts. Hope lifts us out of depression and plants us on firm ground.

According to the tradition of the Miwatani, one of several Sioux warrior societies, a brave warrior would drive a stake in the ground before his enemy. Unless a friend came along to free him, he was obliged to fight or die there.[2]

We need to do the same thing in the Spirit of God. We have to anchor ourselves to something unmoving and make up our minds that we will not leave until the battle is over. The Book of Hebrews says that hope can be this anchor for our souls; it is firm and secure.

"Find rest, O my soul, in God alone; my hope comes from him" (Ps. 62:5). Find hope, and your soul will find rest. Pray *right now* that the Lord will bring great rest into your life. Pray that the Lord will show you how to seek out and discover His hope. Hope and patience are related throughout Scripture. "But if we *hope* for what we do not yet have, we wait for it *patiently*" (Rom. 8:25, emphasis added). Biblical hope, as we have talked about, is maintaining a positive expectation, never giving up but moving toward our God-given goals—even when the outcome of those goals is present only in our hearts. Biblical patience is having strong faith on the inside, despite any lack of movement on the outside.

Sometimes in God's timeline we have to wait, and the waiting may not be for just a few days but may last a season or more. In our Western lifestyle we do not like to wait on anything. We even get bored at long stoplights! We have access to fast food, fast media, fast travel, and just about anything else we can think of. When circumstances occur that are not part of our vision or we experience out-of-the-ordinary delays in seeing our dreams come to pass, what keeps us calm? Patience does. And patience can only be found through taking in the Word of God and responding to it with an obedient heart.

Romans 15:4 says, "Through endurance and the encouragement of the Scriptures we...have hope." The word *endurance* is another way of describing patience. Notice that this scripture also says that we get hope through the "encouragement of the Scriptures." How are you allowing God's Word to encourage you? Beyond church on Sunday, how are you drinking in the Scripture? Whenever we neglect the Word of God, therein lies a big problem. If we are in serious need of hope, a thirty-minute sermon once a week is not enough for us. We simply cannot combat these attacks on our souls through hearing one message. Restoring our hope requires that we spend time with God every day.

I counseled a young woman for several months who had fought a long battle with depression. She constantly asked others to pray for her, but I began to notice that I never saw her pray for herself. I asked her about this, and she told me that she never prayed to God or spent time alone with Him. Her prayer life involved asking other people in the church to pray for her. I let her know that she had to reach out to God and begin to ask Him for healing.

I believe that part of the reason this woman hasn't found healing is because she has never developed a relationship with God herself. She wants to rely on other Christians to do the work for her. Sadly, the last time I talked with her, she was still unwilling to talk with God on her own. She continues to ask others to intercede for her while declining to experience God for herself.

Growing close to the Lord Jesus is not about attending church once a week and asking others to pray for you. If my husband and I only connected one day a week for a short amount of time in a room full of other people, our marriage would start to unravel very quickly. I talk with Kevin every day. He knows everything about me. Jesus wants to be that kind of husband for you. We are, of course, His bride. If we long for intimacy with the Lord, we must invite Him into our daily routine. We must talk with Him and present Him with our requests.

I find that many new believers are unsure about how to connect with the Lord because they do not have any role models to follow. We are to "imitate those who through faith and patience inherit what has been promised" (Heb. 6:12). The people around us influence each of us. The more time we spend around others we want to be like, the easier it is for us to operate in a higher level of hope in the Lord. Hope is contagious! It is one bug that we want to catch. Practice having hope, and focus on becoming a hopeful person. You will not be disappointed. *"And hope does not disappoint us,* because God has poured out his love into our hearts by the Holy Spirit, whom he has given us" (Rom. 5:5, emphasis added).

Become a Dreamer

Hope is closely tied to our dreams. When the devil of depression comes in to steal your hope, the next thing he takes hostage are your dreams. If you have experienced a load of disappointments and unfulfilled desires, it can be difficult to dream again. I cannot promise that all your dreams will come true, but I want you at least to believe that it is *possible* for some of your dreams to reach fulfillment. Dreams are the ideas of our hearts that cause us to believe for things we do not yet have. We have dreams placed in us by the Lord and dreams that we have placed within ourselves. If we can learn to water the ones He gives, then we will reap a huge harvest of the miraculous in our lives.

Man-made dreams require our willpower and energy to keep going, and they will tire us out in the end. Our own dreams are exhausting for us to keep up! The beautiful thing about God-given dreams, however, is that it is up to Him to both raise up the dreams and to fulfill them. For us, the pressure is off. Our only job with regard to the Lord's dreams is to become a dreamer of the impossible and to be obedient to do whatever He places within us. Breathe life into some of the dreams that you have either given up on or never pursued out of fear of disappointment.

The Lord loves dreams, especially *big* dreams. He gave David the dream of becoming king, Paul the dream of preaching to Caesar, Joseph the dream of becoming a mighty leader, Abraham the dream of being a father, Moses the dream of releasing his people from bondage, and the disciples the dream of spreading the gospel to the entire known world. Everyone is born into the world marked with dreams that are longing for fulfillment. We spend a lifetime discovering them all, and that is part of the fun and excitement of living.

If you have given up on your dreams, then you have cut off one of the best parts of life. *Satan comes to steal your dreams, because within the seed of your dreams is your purpose within the kingdom of God.* If the enemy steals your dream, he steals your purpose. Once you lose sight of your purpose, life gets really frustrating.

I have found in my counseling that many depressed women have completely given up on their dreams, believing instead that life is destined to result in one dead dream after another. But dreaming is very important to our souls. This is one way the Lord speaks to us. For example, when my husband lost his job after the economy tanked, he was home for a few months trying to decide what to do next. We talked through a bunch of options such as starting a business, finding another sales job, getting a master's degree. They all sounded like good ideas, but none of them were the right fit. My dad suggested law school to Kevin, and I could tell that at first my husband did not like the idea at all. But then the Lord planted a dream seed into his heart.

Kevin began to think about being a lawyer and dreaming about what it would be like to have his own law practice. Although the Lord never told Kevin in prayer, "Hey, son, go to law school!", He did speak to Kevin through the *dream* of going to law school and by giving him a peace within his heart to do so. It took a step of faith for my husband to apply and interview. The first semester was brutal as he watched half his classmates either fail or drop out. What kept Kevin firmly planted in school? It was the dream of becoming a lawyer. He is now about to be a third-year law student. He is doing amazingly well in school, and he is filled with purpose.

WHAT IS YOUR DREAM?

How do we know when a dream is not from the Lord—when it's a man-made dream? When we are working within our God-given dream, it will fuel us, not drain us. When we are operating in a dream of our own, we will feel burdened, and instead of being energized, we will find ourselves very tired and burned out. We end up serving the dream rather than having the dream serve us. Also, if you have a dream that is outside of what the Word of God allows, then it is certainly not from the Lord. For example, the Lord would never give us the dream of opening a business through underhanded means. His Word will *always* come into agreement with any dream He plants in your heart, not come against it.

Maybe you need to start dreaming for small things such as enjoying the weekend with friends, having a good attitude for the day, or believing that things will get better. Wherever you are starting, the Lord will meet you there. He wants you to *start* dreaming and to allow Him to plant dream seeds within you, starting today. Invite the Lord to plant dreams inside you. Pray that you will know the difference between God-given and man-made dreams in your life.

Open your heart to receiving God's dreams, and allow hope to blossom in you from this day forth. Disappointments will surely knock on your door. And some of them can be really difficult to face. But no matter the disappointment, no matter the trial, fight to keep hope burning within your life. This flame of hope is needed to light your dreams on fire. Depression will always try to steal our hope and our dreams. By restoring hope in our hearts and allowing ourselves to be dreamers, we will wage war against depression and establish the kingdom of God within our hearts.

Dig Deeper

1. What disappointments in your life may have led to you losing hope?

2. What has your hope been in? What do you want your hope to be in?

3. What purpose could the Lord create out of your pain?

4. What dreams have you allowed to die in your life that you believe were God-inspired?

5. What man-made dreams do you need to let go of?

Assignments

Read Psalm 71.

Exercise 1: Find your hope again.

Many times the things we hope for cannot be seen with our human eyes; they can be seen only through the eyes of the Holy Spirit. But "faith is being sure of what we hope for and certain of what we do not see" (Heb. 11:1). List each area of your life in which you have lost hope. Maybe you have lost hope that you will ever have normal emotions, or maybe you have lost hope that you will ever get out of debt. Take time this week to list as many areas as you can think of in which you are running low on hope. After you compile your list, set aside time to pray over each area.

Exercise 2: Become a fearless dreamer.

I made sure to add the word *fearless* to the sentence above, because this exercise is about allowing you to have *big* dreams. As you pray, ask the Lord to reveal dreams to your spirit. Make a dream list for yourself. What are your dreams regarding your family, your career, your future, your spiritual life, your children, your relationships, and your purpose? Once you write these out, spend time praying over your list, and ask the Lord to birth those dreams that have come from Him. Share some of your dreams with your prayer partner, and ask your partner to pray for you to fulfill your dreams.

Prayer time

Pray that the Lord will restore hope inside you. Ask Him to pour hope into your soul, into the forgotten places deep within your heart. Pray that hope will rise up within you to do its work in your life. Invite the Holy Spirit to create hope within you where it has been lost. Thank Him for bringing joy back into your life. Continue to pray these prayers every day. Continually believe that hope is found in the Lord.

> *Lord, My hope comes straight from You and nowhere else. Restore hope in my soul. Replenish the forgotten places of my soul that thirst for hope. I ask that You command hope to rise up and do its full work in my life. I invite You, Holy Spirit, to create hope in the places of my heart where it has been lost and to search out new dreams for me that only You can fulfill. Make me a person filled with hope for my life, my relationships, and those around me. Establish me in true biblical hope, and let it be an anchor to my soul. Amen.*

Chapter 4

SURRENDER EVERYTHING
TO THE LORD

"For I know the plans I have for you," declares the LORD.
—*Jeremiah 29:11*

S OME THINGS ARE super easy for me to surrender. I usually let my husband choose the restaurant when we go out to dinner, not because I'm giving in but because I don't care where we go as much as he does. I enjoy eating anywhere as long as I don't have to fix the meal. I also find it easy to surrender when it comes to the movies we watch. I like true crime, mysteries, and chick flicks. I will be happy with anything in those genres. I didn't choose the car I currently drive, either. I let my husband pick that out, because I don't care what I drive as long as it is air-conditioned and reliable. Kevin likes to research all the "consumer reports," so I figure he can make a good decision.

There are other things that are not so easy for me to surrender. I have a hard time letting friendships go, even when I know I need to. I know I need to work out more, but I haven't yet given in to the discipline that it requires. I sometimes have a hard time saying no, because I really want to please. I am working on giving up my need for approval from others.

ARE YOU SURE, GOD?

Then there is a third level of surrender that requires us to have a spiritual ear that is attuned to God's voice. These surrenders have to do with the mighty callings of God on our lives. The Lord is always gently speaking, asking us to surrender into His hand those things that we hold too tightly against our chests. He asks us to surrender to Him anything that we value more highly than Him. He asks us for every area of our lives in which we still do not trust Him. He sometimes asks for more than we think we can give, in our own strength, at least.

About eight years ago I started a wedding-planning company that I ran in addition to my day job working in the biotech industry. It grew really fast, until I had quickly created a little empire in my local area planning weddings that would blow people away. At the peak of my business I organized twenty-six weddings in one year. That's a whole lot of first dances.

But then God told me to surrender that business. I didn't want to. I liked the extra money I was making. I liked being in charge. And what girl doesn't like flowers, lace, and party food? But God knew I was reaching exhaustion. God knew my husband needed me home on the weekends. God knew I couldn't keep running my business and make the next career move He had in mind for me. As I gave the business up, the Lord opened a door for me in my career and promoted me to another, more specialized company in clinical sales.

At the end of my first year in the new company, I added up how much I had made in bonuses. God has such a sweet sense of humor. The amount I made in bonuses was almost equal to what I would have made if I had kept the wedding-planning business. It was a difference of a few hundred dollars. I learned then that when God says surrender, it is to move us to a better place, prepare us for a new assignment, or cleanse us of something that is keeping us from a closer walk with the Lord.

Either way, surrendering what God asks us to give Him will lead us to our divine destiny. And walking outside of our divine destiny leads to frustration.

We don't like the concept of surrendering because we think it means giving up something that we want. When we played games as a kid and one team quit, it meant that the surrendering team lost. When an army surrenders, it means the other army has won the battle. When we surrender in a court battle, it feels as if we are pleading guilty. No wonder we don't like the word *surrender* very much. Surrendering seems to us like a sign of weakness, and from the time we are young, we are taught to be independent and self-sufficient. Independence and self-sufficiency are not bad qualities, but we can get into trouble when we allow these concepts to get out of balance in our lives.

Of all the requests and commands the Lord has given His people, surely the command to surrender our lives and outcomes to the Lord is the most difficult, because with it there comes a fear of the unknown and the unplanned. Often people who suffer from depression have a history of hurts and wounds that have been caused by careless people or difficult circumstances. *Surrender* can seem like a dirty word, because it means relinquishing our right to have complete control over our future. The worry that most depressed women have is that if they fully relinquish control, then there is a greater possibility for more hurt and disappointment. By maintaining control of the future, they believe their chances of becoming hurt will diminish.

When we assume independence and self-sufficiency to the

point of not needing the Lord, we do not understand the benefits of the relationship we are to have with our heavenly Father. The whole point of walking with God is not only to *allow* Him to take over our future but also to *ask* Him to do it. That may seem like weakness, because it means handing over the outcomes in our lives to another. But we need to remember that the Lord is not a human and can therefore never abuse His position of authority in our lives as a person may do. Although people can be corrupt and fail to have our best interests at heart, our heavenly Father always does what is best for us.

When we are hurt, betrayed, or let down, our first defense is to put up a wall of protection. These walls may take on many forms in our lives and can be so subtle that after a while we do not even realize they are there. The walls just become part of how we function, so when we turn to relate to our heavenly Father, these walls are still in play. We end up treating God as if He were a person we need to protect ourselves from. The truth is, God is nothing like a person, nor does He relate to us in the way people do. Although Jesus became flesh, He still operated fully as God. We do not need walls with God because we do not need protection from His will. He is not going to hurt us.

For some that might be a huge revelation, especially if you have walked through much of your life bearing scars caused by people who were supposed to have loved you. If your earthly father did not quite measure up, you may have found it difficult to understand why a heavenly Father would do much better. But know that God is not a human being, and His ways are everlasting and perfect. *We have entrusted our eternity to Him, and we can entrust our lives to Him as well.* We may feel disappointed at times here on this earth, but one day, when we stand before God with the angels welcoming us home, we will know that He is who He says He is and that He is full of truth and no lies. We will look the Lord in the eye and see the scales of our lives and realize how magnificent His plans for us were. He is truly a loving Father, and He deserves our wholehearted trust and surrender.

God's Plans Are Better than Ours

God is motivated by love for us. *"Because of his great love for us*, God, who is rich in mercy, made us alive with Christ even when we were dead in transgressions"* (Eph. 2:4–5, emphasis added). Our surrender to the Lord is our response to this greatest of loves. Surrender in the biblical sense is not the result of weakness; it is the result of spiritual strength and faith. Making the choice to hand over our lives into God's hands takes a great amount of humility and maturity. Whether we realize it or not, with our every decision and action we all surrender to something. By our own self-will we give in to others, to our own desires, or to the devil's agenda for us. Any of these require the process of surrender.

The truth is, even if we choose not to surrender to the Lord, we still won't have total control over our lives. Life is full of circumstances that we will never have the power to affect, no matter how hard we try. We have a false sense of security when we think we have the reins securely in our hands. Just because we are in the driver's seat does not necessarily mean that we know where we are going or what we will encounter down the road. Our range of sight is so limited compared to the vision that God can see for all eternity.

Think about Peter, one of the disciples, who at the time of Christ's arrest decided, "Hey, this doesn't seem worth it." At that time he had no way of knowing that he would one day be crucified upside down for his faith in Jesus. Then when that day arrived, even as he hung upside down, Peter had no real idea what the blessings in store for him after he breathed his last would be like.

Jesus told Peter, along with the other disciples, that he would one day sit on a throne, standing in judgment over the twelve tribes of Israel during the final judgment of the world (Matt. 19:27–28). Peter, the small-business fisherman from the wrong side of town, the impulsive guy who constantly put his foot in his mouth, would one day judge the tribes of Israel. Wow. When Peter sits on his throne next to the Lord, surely he will say that everything he went through in order to fulfill his purpose in the Lord was worth it.

I can relate to Peter so well. I often open my mouth too soon, get overly emotional about things, and am a little rough around the edges. I doubt that in his pre-disciple days, as Peter brought in his catch of fish each morning, having an aching back and salt-covered skin, he ever imagined he would one day sit in a place of authority next to the Son of God and bless or condemn the tribes of Israel. Peter was a flawed man who came to know the perfect Savior. Our flaws, like Peter's, can be made beautiful in the Lord. See, God had laid out a supernatural plan for Peter before his birth, and He has in place a supernatural plan for us as well, even though we may not be able to see it right now.

Surrender is the integral ingredient to fulfilling the purpose and plan of God for our lives. Our decision making is limited to what we can see in front of us. That is why we desperately need the Holy Spirit to speak to us and to make decisions for us. Even if we try our very hardest to make good choices, the Lord alone knows where every road leads and what lies around each bend. We do not know the future—only God does. But the Lord will never ambush us and force His desires over ours.

Only as we choose to surrender to the Lord do we allow Him the freedom to control our present and our future.

One reason people suffer from depression is because they want control over the outcomes of situations in their lives but just can't seem to get that control. Realize that handing over control of your life to the Lord *will result in something far better than you could have come up with on your own.* What I am trying to say is that we get a much better deal when we allow God to take over.

What good is the power of control without the wisdom to handle it? And we don't have that wisdom! Wisdom is found only in God, not in ourselves (James 1:5). Insisting on our own way can be a full-time job if we let it, because we never quite arrive at a place of complete happiness. There will always be another option out there beckoning us to the mirage of self-fulfillment. It tells us to feed our desires and ignore everything else. So is there a better way?

SURRENDER HAS ITS REWARDS

Jesus asks us to completely abandon ourselves to the will of the Father. Amazingly, though, He didn't just give us this command and then fail to do it Himself. "Although he was a son, he learned *obedience* from what he suffered" (Heb. 5:8, emphasis added). Jesus, the Son of God, had to learn obedience through surrender while He was in His flesh here on earth. He had to do it so we could see that through His righteousness we too can surrender all and learn how to walk in obedience to the Father. Surrender and obedience are mutually inclusive. We cannot have one without the other. Obedience is what we are asked to do in the *present*. Surrender is turning over the *future* outcome of events in our lives to the Lord.

The Lord does not ask us to surrender our everything to

Him and give us no promises in return. He responds to our yielding by saying that He will lead us into our divine destiny both on this earth and in heaven. I think that is a great deal. If you struggle with giving God the plans for your life, pray that the Lord will open your heart to the concept of biblical surrender. Pray that you will reach total abandonment to the will of God.

Psalm 119:32 says, "I run in the path of your commands, for you have set my heart free." In other words, God says that if we surrender our will and decide to follow His commands, He will make sure that we walk with complete freedom in our hearts. If you are suffering from depression and anxiety, take note of this beautiful verse. It is a promise from the Lord especially to you. If you run toward God and in the path of His commands, He will set your heart free from bondage. The ultimate consequence of following our own path is that the road we are walking on will crumble beneath our feet. But the ultimate blessing in surrendering to God's plan is living a life of great rest in Him.

Great peace can be found in the very *act* of surrender. I was in a car accident in 2006 that left my back in pretty bad shape. Unfortunately I now deal with chronic pain every day because a woman ran a stop sign as she was looking for her doctor's office. I have a hard time driving, flying on planes, and sitting in chairs for long periods of time. The pain affects my sleep almost every night, and I have to do quite a bit of stretching every morning just to be able to turn my head. Even as I type this paragraph, my back is radiating pain. For a long time I was very angry with God over all this. Years of pain...Why had that woman run a stop sign that day? Why had God not healed me?

I had it out with the Lord one day for about seven hours. I

was home in bed, flat on my back, and I had been lying on my heating pad for so long that I'd about had it. I cried to God; I pleaded with Him; I probably even threatened. After my all-day tantrum, I was exhausted. It was at that moment that I finally gave up and told God that even if He never healed me, I was not going to be angry anymore or let this pain ruin me. I had cried enough tears and spent way too much energy feeling sorry for myself. So I decided to let my disappointment and anger go. It did not happen all at once, but over the next few weeks, I began to see a change. My pain was still the same, but my attitude was being healed.

I no longer harbor any resentment toward the Lord or the woman who ran the stop sign. I do want to be healed, and believe me, I still pray for healing to come, but I am at rest, no matter how much this back of mine makes me suffer. And that is the beauty of abandonment. This injury has been surrendered to the Lord. It is now His to do with what He wants. I can be at peace even with a back that isn't. Peace is a by-product of my obedience. Unrest always goes hand in hand with disobedience.

Do you live a life of peace or unrest? Could the state of your heart be directly related to your obedience or disobedience in following God?

God's Plans for Us Are Good

"And this is love: that we walk in *obedience* to his commands. As you have heard from the beginning, his command is that you walk in love" (2 John 1:6, emphasis added). Obedience to God will always lead us to walk in love, which the Lord explicitly taught His disciples to do (John 15:12). And the reason Jesus taught us to love one another is that God loved us first— far more than we even realize!

We somehow have this crazy idea that if we were to surrender everything to God, He would soon enough ask us to sell everything we own, leave our families, and move to a foreign country to serve Him. It's as if we don't trust God to come up with a good plan for our lives that will suit our giftings. We fear that He will ask us for more than we can give and require us to do something we have no desire to do. And that is exactly what Satan wants us to believe. But because God loves us, His plans for us are good.

Satan knows that if every Christian in the world were to totally abandon his own will and to walk purely in the will of the Father, the entire earth would be shaken from its foundation with the fullness of God's presence. Can you imagine what would happen? All of us walking in our divine destiny all at once—it would be amazing.

But an overwhelming majority of believers will continue to buy into Satan's propaganda and therefore never reach their potential. The idea of total abandonment to the Father seems completely crazy to them, so they never even try it out.

So what *does* happen when we throw off the restraints of our will and allow the Lord to take the driver's seat? You will never know what it means for *your* life until you hand over the keys to the car. Psalm 23 is one of the most quoted verses in all of Scripture. It describes the heart of the Lord toward His children. Let's take a look at it: "The LORD is my shepherd, I shall not be in want. He makes me lie down in green pastures, he leads me beside quiet waters, he restores my soul" (vv. 1–3). In essence, God is describing the plans He has for those who give Him full authority to lead. The Lord Jesus is described as our Shepherd in many places throughout Scripture to paint a picture for us of His constant attention to His flock.

When we following the Shepherd, the Lord brings us to

places of provision—just as a shepherd leads his sheep to beautiful green fields that will satisfy the flock's needs. He then makes sure that we drink of the quiet waters in the river of life, and He promises that in addition to meeting our needs, He will also restore our broken souls. All the sheep have to do is follow. See, God *leads* us into this good place. He does not push us. The Holy Spirit *always* leads. If we feel pushed, it is usually not the Lord speaking but the devil.

The Shepherd always has *good* intentions, not bad ones. He knows where the best pastureland is and where the winding brooks of water flow. He knows what we need, and He desires to bring us into our divine destiny. "'For I know the plans I have for you,' declares the LORD, 'plans to prosper you and not to harm you, plans to give you hope and a future'" (Jer. 29:11).

When Surrender Is Hard

Surrendering to the will of the Father is easy when it requires no faith, keeps us comfortable, or fits neatly into the plans we have for our own lives. As we grow in maturity with the Lord, we will find that surrendering to the Word of God is often fairly easy, because we love Him and understand His intentions. It is really fun and easy to walk in the green pastures of God's good will.

But what if we have to walk through a desert to arrive there? How do we handle that? Let's take a look at the lives of Jonah and Abraham as they trekked through their desert paths in search of green pastureland. As they discovered, the more quickly we reach obedience in the desert, the faster we will be led into our promised land. (See an example of this in Numbers 32:13–22.) We have plenty of biblical examples that teach us that very principle.

Jonah is the famous biblical character who was in the belly

of a whale for three days before being spit out and delivered to safety. Although commonly depicted as a kids' cartoon, this real-life story is so much more than a sweet children's bedtime book. Jonah was a prophet who was asked by the Lord to deliver a message to a very evil people in the city of Nineveh: "The word of the LORD came to Jonah son of Amittai: 'Go to the great city of Nineveh and preach against it, because its wickedness has come up before me.' But Jonah ran away from the LORD" (Jon. 1:1–3).

Since Jonah was a prophet, I imagine that this was not the first time the Lord had spoken to him. Maybe Jonah had always done what the Lord had requested of him up until this point. But something about this particular assignment made Jonah decide that he did not want to obey God's call. Maybe Nineveh was such a wicked city that Jonah feared for his life. Getting up in front of an entire city to call out their sins is not exactly the way to make new friends. Or perhaps Jonah did not want to make the long trip to the city. It would mean leaving his family behind and traveling by himself. Or maybe the sins of the city were so disgusting to him that he just did not want the people to receive any grace. Read the entire Book of Jonah, and you will see that the prophet was upset that the Lord showed so much compassion to the people of Nineveh.

Whatever the reason, Jonah didn't want to go, so he caught an outbound ship and tried to outrun God. As the ship sailed, a violent storm arose and threatened the safety of the boat and its passengers. Jonah convinced the crew that it was due to his behavior toward God, and he told them to throw him overboard into the sea. If you ever attended Sunday school as a child, you will know the next part of the story. Jonah was swallowed by a large fish, and only after he surrendered to God's will was he was delivered and spit out onto dry land.

Upon vowing to be obedient, Jonah's life was spared. Jonah continued to Nineveh and delivered the message that the Lord had given him. "When God saw what they did and how they turned from their evil ways, he had compassion and did not bring upon them the destruction he had threatened" (Jon. 3:10).

It took some time in the "desert" for Jonah to finally obey God's command. But the Lord had great mercy on Jonah, and He forgave him for running away from his call. An entire city could have experienced complete devastation if Jonah had not walked in obedience. As He did with Jonah, sometimes the Lord will allow a storm to come into our lives so that we will repent for disobedience and surrender our will to Him.

The story of Abraham is full of examples of the blessings that come with surrender as well as the consequences that come with disobedience. Before the Lord ever spoke through the prophets or had even recorded any of His Word, He came to a man named Abram. Abram, or Abraham, as he was later to be called, was chosen by God to become the father of God's special people. God made a covenant with Abraham and promised him a family so big that it would be like the sands of the sea. (The Lord, of course, held to His promise, and eventually Jesus was born out of Abraham's lineage. Now all believers in Christ are part of Abraham's family, the family of faith; the blood of Jesus has grafted us in.) After God gave Abraham this promise, however, Abraham and his wife Sarah waited many years for the promise to be fulfilled. Out of desperation to have a child, Abraham had a son with his maidservant. As you can imagine, that was not such a good idea.

Finally, in His own perfect time, God fulfilled His promise to Abraham when Sarah give birth to a baby boy, whom his parents named Isaac. Isaac was the apple of his father's eye. I'm sure his mother was overly protective of him. She had prayed for so long to have a child that I bet she didn't want him out of her sight. This was a blessed and happy family. They finally had their son, the one who would fulfill God's promise and pass on the lineage of Abraham. Finally everything was going according to plan.

But here comes the desert part: "Some time later God tested Abraham. He said to him, 'Abraham!' 'Here I am,' he replied. Then God said, 'Take your son, your only son, Isaac, whom you love, and go to the region of Moriah. Sacrifice him there as a burnt offering on one of the mountains I will tell you about'" (Gen. 22:1–2).

Surrender can be a terribly hard thing for us to do, especially when it comes to surrendering our loved ones into the hands and will of God. Parents have a hard time stepping back and allowing the Holy Spirit to be the final authority over a child's life, whether the child is five years old or forty. I bet Abraham's walk up the hill of Moriah was excruciatingly long for the father and his son. You know that he wanted to cry, scream, or run away from what God was asking of him. But he chose surrender. Abraham did indeed ascend to the top of the mountain, tie up his son, and raise his knife over him.

"But the angel of the LORD called out to him from heaven, 'Abraham! Abraham!' 'Here I am,' he replied. 'Do not lay a hand on the boy,' he said. 'Do not do anything to him. Now I know that you fear God, because you have not withheld from me your son, your only son'" (Gen. 22:11–12).

Sometimes it is not so much *what* God asks us to do that is important—sometimes He just wants to see if we will be obedient to Him. If you are fighting God's plans, I challenge you to stop struggling and embrace God's will. The process of surrendering can seem overwhelming at first, but we are not alone in it. The precious Holy Spirit, our great Comforter, will hold our hands the entire time. His route toward our promised land may include a few desert paths on the way, but the journey is worth it. Following Jesus is truly the most exciting adventure. We don't know exactly what's coming next, but we know that His will for us will be made complete. He is a good Father who gives good gifts. Don't you just love getting presents? "Every good and perfect gift is from above, coming down from the Father of the heavenly lights" (James 1:17).

Emotional problems can feel overwhelming and keep us from seeing God's goodness. Instead of surrendering to depression, decide to surrender to God's plans. It may take walking through a desert to get to your green pasture, but don't give up. Keep following the Good Shepherd.

Dig Deeper

1. Do you have any storms or "big fish" in your life due to an unwillingness to surrender to the Lord? If so, what are they?

2. Do you have any emotional walls up? How could emotional walls affect your relationship with God?

3. What does surrendering to God mean?

Assignments

Exercise 1: Make an obedience list.

I believe that every Christian can hear the voice of God. If you are a believer, He has spoken to you about things that He would like you to be obedient in doing. Many times we don't realize that what we hear is actually the Lord speaking, so we put off what He is asking us to do. Maybe you need to make amends with a friend or break away from a relationship that is unhealthy. He may be calling you to a job change or asking you to get out of debt.

Make a list of the things the Lord has been speaking to you about doing but that you have not yet taken action on. As you work on your list, ask God to reveal to you those things that He has asked of you. Pray that the Holy Spirit will cause you to remember specific details. Once you have made your list, go through each thing the Lord is asking of you, and tell the Lord how you will be obedient to Him. Pray that the Lord will strengthen you to obey. Make a plan to take action on each of these items, and talk about your plans with your prayer partner.

Exercise 2: Ask the Lord to show you what you have not surrendered to Him, and prayerfully abandon your will to His.

If you ask the Lord what He wants you to surrender, He will tell you. But then you have to be ready and willing to give Him the things that He shows you. Seek the Lord concerning this exercise. You will need supernatural strength to surrender your life and all that it entails into the hands of the Lord. Approach the throne of God in boldness and tell Him that you want to surrender to Him your desires, both present and future.

Prayer time

Once you have surrendered your life into God's hands, then surrender your family and all of your relationships to Him. Surrender is not a one-time action. We have to surrender in some way to the Lord on a daily basis. Make this decision to surrender a part of your time with the Lord each day, spending time releasing all of yourself into His hands. In prayer surrender your spouse, your children, your career, your plans for

ure, your finances, your home and possessions, your
s, your need for healing—all of your needs. Lay them
all at the foot of the cross, and ask the Lord to bless them all
within His will.

*Lord, I have tried for far too long to control my life,
and today I surrender all of myself to You. I relinquish having to always know what direction my life
will take. Instead I choose to be at peace because
You are in the driver's seat of my tomorrow. I surrender always having to know the "why" behind
Your decisions. I trust You completely, and I will
praise Your name no matter what happens to me. I
believe You can be trusted and that You will always
do what's best for me. I surrender my spouse, my
children, my career, my plans for the future, my
finances, my home and possessions, my parents,
and my need for healing. I am totally in Your hands,
and that is the very best place for me to be. Thank
You for paying attention to every detail of my life. I
love You, Jesus. Amen.*

Chapter 5

TAKE A MORAL INVENTORY

Who may ascend the hill of the Lord? Who may stand in his holy place? He who has clean hands and a pure heart.
—*Psalm 24:3–4*

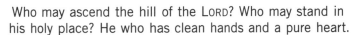

M Y HUSBAND AND I have an amazing backyard, although it was not always that way. At one point we had tried to sell our house, and while feedback on the house was great, we heard over and over that our house would be perfect for a family if only there were a backyard for kids to play in. We knew this was true, but at the time we didn't have pets or kids, so the lack of a backyard didn't bother us a bit. The land behind our house sloped down, and the entire back of the property was covered with thick Alabama woods that were impossible to walk through because of the overgrown brush. The real estate agents kept telling us that our backyard (more like a back-overgrown-mess) was useless, but I thought it was pretty to look at. It also provided a shield between us and the neighbors, and the trees kept the house shaded.

Then one day we needed the yard to be useful. It all started with a stray dog I saw one Thanksgiving Day. She was so neglected and pitiful that I convinced Kevin to put her in the back of our Trailblazer and bring her home. Then came another rescue, then another. Suddenly we had three dogs and a rather pitiful backyard for them to run around in.

Thus "project backyard" began. It took an entire team to clear out the small trees, brush, and briars. What we ended up with was a shockingly massive backyard that was rather park-like. We kept the large trees and had room around them for a good-sized grassy area. We sweated as we completed the rest of the work: up went the fence, a patio, a custom dog kennel. Soon we had ourselves one amazing backyard fit for our puppies and future kiddos. By removing the unnecessary undergrowth, we transformed our unusable space into a yard that even *Southern Living* would have been proud of. That beautiful yard had been there all the time; we simply needed to rid it of the undergrowth to find that out.

Dealing With Sin From the Inside Out

It is amazing how removing can sometimes be more powerful than adding. A great many Christians spend a lot of time adding good things to their lives yet never consider what needs to be taken out. Depressed people often believe that happiness would come if only this or that could be added to their lives. This creates an "if only" thought process. If only I had more money. If only my kids were better behaved. If only God would answer my prayers. This kind of thinking keeps us focused on the external things that we lack rather than on internal issues that need to be addressed. But by removing the sin that puts limits on our faith, we can create an atmosphere in our hearts that will enable deep inner healing to take place.

The Lord desires His children to be mature and holy, fit workers in the kingdom of God. Sin, however, crowds our lives in such a way that it limits our effectiveness within the kingdom of God. The weeds of sin will tie us up, choke out the better plants, and steal our future. If we are going to reach our destiny in the Lord, we must strive to walk with clean hands and a pure heart. Sin must be removed from our lives in order for freedom to completely take over. Freedom in Jesus and devotion to sin cannot occupy the same space within our hearts. There is room for only one master.

David wrote, "For troubles without number surround me; my sins have overtaken me, and I cannot see. They are more than the hairs of my head, and my heart fails within me" (Ps. 40:12). He understood that sin keeps us bound to our past, brings shame upon our todays, and will visit destruction on our tomorrows. It is in our best interest to heed the call of repentance. In fact, this call was so important to the heart of God that it was the message He gave to John the Baptist when the prophet lived in the desert.

For four hundred years before John the Baptist's time, God's prophets had been silent. The prophet Malachi had been the last to record the word of the Lord, and I am sure the people of Israel wondered if the Lord's voice would ever be heard again. Then the Lord chose prophet John to break centuries of silence and usher in the Messiah: "In those days John the Baptist came, preaching in the Desert of Judea and saying, '*Repent*, for the kingdom of heaven is near'" (Matt. 3:1–2, emphasis added).

God broke His silence with a message of the people's need for repentance. As John's ministry reached its climax, Jesus came to the river where John had been baptizing. Many in Israel had turned their hearts toward repentance and received baptism through John's ministry in preparation for the coming of the Lord. Jesus Himself was then baptized by John and afterward was led into the desert to be tempted by the devil for forty days.

After He came out of the wilderness, Jesus began to preach. And what were His first sermons about? "From that time on Jesus began to preach, '*Repent*, for the kingdom of heaven is near'" (Matt. 4:17, emphasis added). The Lord began His ministry by teaching on repentance, just as John had. The Father wanted the people to have clean hearts—hearts that were able and ready to receive the good news of the kingdom.

God Is Not Mad at Us

My husband grew up in a church that placed great emphasis on sin, hell, and being punished for your trespasses—not exactly a message I would be dying to hear week after week. Although the minister had good intentions, this message made the people "sin conscious" and not "grace conscious." Lists of offenses that would get a person into trouble were repeated to the congregation. If a man had long hair, he could be sentenced to hell, and tattoos would consign anyone to eternal torment. One slip, it seemed, and you could be on your way to eternal misery in no time.

All this left my husband feeling as if he could never be a real Christian—that he was too imperfect. The list of offenses and the implications of damnation drove him away from the cross instead of to it. He walked away from God as a teenager, because he was never fed the full truth of the Word of God concerning sin. Many years later, now that he has gained an understanding of God's love and grace, my husband walks in freedom, believing in and following Jesus. So what is the part of the story that he had been missing as a youth? We see it in Romans 2:4: "God's kindness leads you toward repentance."

It is God's kindness and fatherly love that bring us to true repentance. If only all Christians throughout history would have known and operated within this principle. It would have caused many more to come to repentance, I believe, and changed the very course of history. How many Christians try to lead others to Jesus through the kindness of the Father?

I remember learning how to "share the gospel" during high school using visual teaching methods. I don't remember anything about the kindness of God being expressed in it. Arguments in favor of Christianity do not usually produce a harvest, and, in fact, they often do more harm than good. Fear may change a person's behavior, but it has no ability to change the heart.

It saddens me when churches teach mainly on the sinfulness of humanity and pay little attention to the loving grace of God. Instead of developing a pure heart in people, this scare tactic leaves the followers of God in fear of displeasing the Lord. Sin consciousness breeds a lifestyle of fear in which the Christian does good simply out of apprehension rather than out of love for the Father. *It is possible for a person to do good but actually to be very far from God.* The Father is much more concerned with the motives of our *hearts* than He is with our behavior itself. For if the heart is pure, right behavior will surely follow. A congregation of people who don't sin outwardly is displeasing to God if there is strife, envy, condemnation, and unclean thoughts inside their hearts. One day, when we stand before the Father, any good action we have done that was not motivated simply by love for God will be burned in the fire as dross.

I can think of so many good things I have done that were generated from wretched motives. Perhaps I acted because I wanted others to think well of me or to win approval from my peers. When a good act is prompted by a wrong motive, it's an act of sin and rebellion against the Lord. At best these kinds of deeds are meaningless before God. Thank the Lord that He can set us free of these useless "good" works and put a new purpose in our hearts. When pleasing Him becomes our focus, the sins we struggle with can be overcome. Not only will we be set free from sin, but we will begin to be delivered from depression as well. When our hearts are focused on pleasing the Lord, we are left with little time to feel sorry for ourselves.

Jesus spoke frequently in His earthly ministry on this aspect of sin. He knew that religious men would end up with a sin-conscious mind-set if the love of God was not first in their hearts. These religious leaders who lived in Jesus's day are around today as well. *But empty religion, which is always quick to point out our areas of sin, offers us no power to overcome these sins.* Without the power of the Lord intervening in our need, we are left to try and overcome sin by our own efforts. The Pharisees and Sadducees loved to burden the people with their lists of dos and don'ts, while Jesus pointed out that the leaders themselves had hearts that were full of wrong. Concerning them, Jesus told the people, "Do not do what they do, for they do not practice what they preach. They tie up heavy loads and put them on men's shoulders, but they themselves are not willing to lift a finger to move them" (Matt. 23:3–4).

Certainly these words were received as radical when Jesus said them. The very foundation of the religious Jewish system had been founded on the laws of God, which were good. But the Jewish priests enforced a reward system that worked according to the people's actions rather than the intent of their hearts. Besides adhering to God's 613 laws that were written throughout the first five books of the Old Testament, the religious leaders had more than six thousand pages (yes, that's a lot!) of additional rules they called the oral law that spelled out details of every specific sin—way beyond what the Lord had decreed in the Scripture.[1]

So How Does Repentance Work?

The law of God was written by the Lord not to bind us but for our benefit, to show all of humanity our need for a Savior. It was meant to be used as a plumb line (Amos 7:8) to reveal to us our sin so that we would look to God for righteousness. Ultimately when we use God's law to guide us, it should always point us to the cross, for we can never become righteous enough in our own strength to please God. Only when we take on righteousness *through* Jesus will we ever be able to stand in His presence.

Religion tells us that *we* must carry the burden of overcoming the sin in our lives. Let the following allegory about carrying sin and trying to release it in our own power speak to your heart.

> *There is a lovely path before me, and yet I often venture off this path when something alongside it catches my attention. With each wandering, I feel an increasing pressure collecting on my shoulders. Soon enough the pressure becomes a huge and heavy pack. It is left to me alone to carry, and I tire as the journey becomes long. The pack becomes so heavy that I become sore; it rubs me raw with each step forward that I take. When I fall, I must rise on my own, mustering the strength to push upward. With the passing of time, the burden becomes part of me. I must adjust how I walk in order to accommodate the pack. But finally I can take no more. I wrestle to pull the pack from my back as I scream with anger. As I tug and pull, the cords are too strong for me.*
>
> *I look toward others around me with wide eyes and beg them to help carry my burden. "Take it away!" I scream. I fight, but when the strength of my pack is tested, it is proven too difficult to remove. Resisting it becomes*

utterly useless. Tears stream down my face, but the pack remains in place.

In the far distance I see a man walking toward me. "My beloved," he calls out. He sees the pack and the tears it has caused. As he reaches me, he lovingly unties each string that held the pack in place; he pulls out a key that easily unlocks each of the locks holding my burden together. He then lifts the pack off my back, and for the first time I am able to stand up straight.

I think at first that the man is going to lay my pack on the ground, but then I see his muscles begin to strain as he lifts it upon his own back. I call out, "Oh no, please, sir, it is I who must carry this burden! It is for my own sins!" He just smiles, and after the pack is firmly placed on his back, he reaches into his pocket to pull out healing balm. He knows where each sore and each strained muscle on my body is. He takes his time and addresses each of my wounds gently. I take a deep breath, and I realize that the pain from my journey is not so great as it was.

The man collects each of my fallen tears into a vessel and wipes away those that remain along my cheeks. He kisses me on the forehead, as if he were a loving daddy. Suddenly I am aware of his beautiful, radiant clothing, and I realize that I am wearing rags. The man senses my embarrassment and then drapes me in a cloak of beautiful colors. I am about to tell him that I am unworthy of this beautiful garment and to confess to him that I have wandered off the path, but he senses what I plan to say and tells me, "I am doing this because I love you, my beloved. I always have." He looks me straight in the eye, and at once my hands become clean, and so do my feet, which had been dirty from the journey's walk.

The man turns to turn to leave, and I am gripped with fear. "Oh, please, sir, don't leave me. What am I to do?" I remember the weight of the pack and think of the journey ahead, and my heart races with the thought of continuing ahead without this man. "Fear not," he says. "I will send my Spirit to walk with you." At once a great wind blows my hair, and my new robe dances in the air. I sense this holy wind blowing me onward in the path ahead. Every time the wind comes, I walk in the direction it blows. I walk with little effort now. I can barely remember my former walk, for it seems so far behind me now.

I realize that the man is no longer in sight, but I feel as if he is near me still. His words fill all my senses. "My beloved," he had called me. One moment with this man, and I have changed. I no longer wander off the path. It is now easy to stay on course with the wind blowing me along.

"Come to me, all you who are weary and burdened, and I will give you rest. Take my yoke upon you and learn from me, for I am gentle and humble in heart, and you will find rest for your souls. For my yoke is easy and my burden is light" (Matt. 11:28–30).

Jesus does not ask us to carry the sin that He already conquered. Jesus comes along and lifts our burdens of sin and heaviness from our backs and puts them on His. He then cleanses our wounds and blows His living Spirit into our very breath. Once we learn to walk on the path laid before us *with* and *in* Him (see John 14:17), the journey of life in Christ becomes both easy and light. And that, my friend, is the secret to overcoming depression as well. We must trust that as we do our part in walking toward freedom, God will surely do His. The work of overcoming is completely in His hands. The beginning and end of our freedom lie in His supernatural power. This power is not found in religious circles, well-meaning books, secular counseling, or prescription meds. It is found only in Him.

When Jesus lifts the burden of sin from our backs, in return He asks us to take His yoke upon us. A yoke is a tool that links two animals together so that they can plow a field or accomplish some other type of work. Usually a younger, untrained beast is put in a yoke with an older one that has had many seasons of plowing and harvesting in its experience. When the younger beast under the yolk becomes frightened and tries to pull away or tries to pull ahead too quickly, the experienced animal under the yoke steadies the younger one. The younger learns to follow the pace and direction of the older or risks the frustration of trying to walk outside the tried and proven path.

Jesus asks us to become yoked with Him so that we may learn from His movements, from His pace. As we stay beside Him in His yoke, then with the passing of each season, we assuredly become more and more like the Lord until our movements mirror His. When we focus on maintaining our pace with the Lord as our guide, it becomes easy for us to receive correction and to release the behaviors that pull us out of step with the Master. When our full attention is on Jesus instead of on our sin, it is much easier for us to embrace a lifestyle of grace and obedience.

Yes, the Lord asks us to walk in holiness, but His love for us is not based on our willingness to be yoked with Him. We must understand that it is not our actions that make God love us. He loves us despite our sinful ways and despite our battles with depression. We may think that the battles we are in are proof that God has turned His back on us or forgotten us. But that is far from the truth. The Bible says that God is close to the brokenhearted (Ps. 34:18). He loved us before we ever knew or even acknowledged Him. Sin is very ugly to God, but we are very beautiful to Him.

If We Really Love God...

John 14:15 is a tough verse for me to swallow: "If you love me, you will obey what I command." It confronts me with the truth about God's love: if I do not follow the Lord, I am saying to my Father that I do not love Him as I should.

It is the Father's love for us, however, that will give us the desire to please Him—to love Him back. The answer to any sin issue in our lives is always the presence of the Lord. The more our lives revolve around loving the Lord, the more aware we become of grieving Him when we sin. Allow these truths to sink into your heart. Not only will the love of the Father give us new desires, but also living in the love of the Father will allow us to walk in perfect peace. The presence of Jesus chases out the darkness of depression and loneliness.

If we are walking in sin but do not think about it or realize how it grieves the Lord, then we are not close enough to Him. Think about it this way: If we hurt our best friend with a comment we make, most of the time we can immediately tell that the person is wounded by our words. Our friend's tone of voice changes, or maybe she tries to get off the phone quickly. Our friend doesn't act typically the next time we get together. We are aware that something has changed, and it puts distance between us. Only when we acknowledge our hurtful words and apologize is the relationship mended. On the other hand, if we hurt someone we barely know, many times we may not realize it until someone tells us what we have done. We do not know the person well enough to notice the rift we have created.

In the same way, the closer we come to the Lord, the more

we will learn to recognize those times when we have wounded the Holy Spirit by our sin. God wants us to be concerned about the Spirit's desires: "Those who live according to the sinful nature have their minds set on what that nature desires; but those who live in accordance with the Spirit have their minds set on what the Spirit desires" (Rom. 8:5).

You may be thinking, "God wounded by people? How can that be? He is God—how can our actions cause Him hurt?" It is in these very questions that we can really see how much God loves us. He *chooses* to love us. Like God, we can be hurt only by something or someone we care about or love. It is because of God's crazy, radical, overwhelming love for us that the Creator allows Himself to be grieved by His creation. But still, we can never sin too much to lose the Lord's affection for us. He remains faithful even when we do not.

Don't Let Bad Fruit Grow

When we have sinned, our first response should be to ask for and receive forgiveness through Jesus. The Father cannot pardon us if we do not accept His gift of grace and salvation.

Second, we must learn to recognize areas of sin within our lives. The closer we get to the Lord, the easier it is for us to identify sin within ourselves. God shows us through His Word the things that are displeasing to Him, and He speaks to us about these things through the Holy Spirit. In addition to this the Lord has put into each member of humanity a conscience. "Conscience" is actually what the world calls it—that gut feeling we have that lets us know when something is not quite right. This feeling is really the person of the Holy Spirit speaking to us, showing us the difference between good and evil and pointing us toward righteousness.

God has shown all humanity what Paul calls "God's

invisible qualities": "For since the creation of the world God's invisible qualities—his eternal power and divine nature—have been clearly seen, being understood from what has been made, so that men are without excuse" (Rom. 1:20). One of these invisible qualities is knowing right from wrong.

Any time we step farther away from God and toward sin, our conscience can become muddled, and we are no longer able to get that check in our spirit when we are walking in the wrong direction. The first time we walk into a particular sin, we might feel sick to our stomachs, nervous because we know we shouldn't be doing what we are doing. But perhaps we decide to go ahead and try it anyway, pushing away the thought of consequences. The second time we still may feel a little sick, but we did it once before, so we think maybe it isn't that bad. The next time it gets even easier. That is how sin takes root in our lives. It starts as a seed—something small, an idea planted by the enemy.

For most people, depression starts as a small seed. An event, hurt, or wound was planted in our hearts. Even if the hurt seems awful to us, in its seed form we really cannot realize all the disaster it can potentially bring. Usually the seed is in a pretty package and looks small enough for us to handle. We think we can always get rid of it if we want to; it is just a tiny seed. But once we say yes to the new bloom and welcome it, the seed is planted securely. Unless we pull it out, it will be watered by our sinful thoughts and actions. We are always actively watering things in our lives—either sin or the things of God. Whatever we water will grow; whatever we do not water will die within us.

A seed of sin comes in as many forms, as do dark thoughts. Once this seed starts to take root, it becomes demanding. It requires something of us, and it always takes more than we really want to give. It grows and grows until it produces fruit in our lives. What may have started as a small planting has the potential power to rule over us. Depression is like this. If it is watered and allowed to grow within us, the fruit of depression will spread deadly vines, choking out the healthy portions of our lives. The fruit of sin comes when sin is fully grown and has had its way within us. The deeper the roots and the larger the planting, the more difficult sin is to relinquish from our lives.

It is far easier to remove sin when it is not fully grown. We should not wait to remove it; as soon as we identify it, we should be willing to uproot it from our lives. The more room there is for sin in our lives, the less room there is for the Lord. He will not compete for our attention. He is God above all and deserves all our affection.

Consider what these verses have to say about the kind of fruit God wants to see growing in our lives:

> Produce fruit in keeping with repentance.
> —LUKE 3:8

> No good tree bears bad fruit, nor does a bad tree bear good fruit.
> —LUKE 6:43

> I am the vine; you are the branches. If a man remains in me and I in him, he will bear much fruit; apart from me you can do nothing.
> —JOHN 15:5

> This is to my Father's glory, that you bear much fruit, showing yourselves to be my disciples.
> —JOHN 15:8

Just as we can bear lovely fruit from the Lord, so we can also bear fruit from the devil. This second kind of fruit is ugly, full of empty promises from the enemy. Sin will always have an effect on us. We cannot sow ungodly seed without reaping ungodly fruit from it. Only Jesus can come along and pull out these evil plantings by their roots and burn them in the fire. If we try to uproot them by ourselves without the power of God, we may get the stem, but the root will remain. If the root remains, then as soon as it finds nourishment, it will begin to grow once more. That is why we can have the best of intentions and still not be able to do the right thing. Until the root of bad fruit is gone, the thing still has potential to spring right back up again.

Let God Do the Work

We can try to overcome sin in our own power for a season, but we will eventually get weary. "I am not going to act like that again!" we tell ourselves. But the next time we are tempted, we find ourselves right back where we were before. This leads to exhaustion. Going around and around the same mountain of sin over and over will wear us out and make us believe that our sin is impossible for us to overcome.

Overcoming sin by ourselves *is* impossible. We were not made with the ability to do it on our own. Under the old covenant the Israelite priests had to sacrifice animals for the people's sin and ask for the atonement of God on the people's behalf. People today still cannot become spotless without God doing His part. Our part is to supply a true, repentant heart along with faith to turn away from our sin. God must then supply His supernatural power for the overcoming of sin in our lives made possible through Jesus's death on the cross. We can cover our sin up, dress it up, pretend it's not there—and still it remains. That is why we must have Jesus. He alone can remove sin altogether. He alone can uproot the weeds sown into our hearts and plant in their place the flowers of the Spirit of God.

We must look at overcoming sin in a new way. It is not about human willpower, positive thinking, or trying really hard. It is about inviting God to change us from the inside out. It is about asking Him to remove, burn up, and kill everything inside us that is unfit for the kingdom of God. We must be willing to give up anything that is unpleasing to our heavenly Father, and instead of running away from God when we have sin in our lives, we must run to Him with our problem.

Paul reminds us in Romans 8:1 that "there is now no condemnation for those who are in Christ Jesus." We are to live free of shame from our past iniquities. We must not let condemnation keep us from the throne of God when we are struggling in sin. Sin literally binds us like handcuffs, keeping us from the best that the Lord has for us. The world would say that purity is outdated, too draining to maintain, unfit for today's standards, and plain boring. That is exactly what Satan would have us believe. He does not want us to realize that a sinless life brings freedom to our souls and opens the doors to the kingdom of God in our lives.

Many Christians want God's power to change, but they are not willing to seek godly purity. The Father will not empower those who hold on to their sin, but He will never withhold Himself from the life that is surrendered to Him. He takes great delight in obedience and always blesses the pure in heart. It is in His nature to give freely of His Spirit to the forgiven and blameless. For "blessed are the pure in heart, for they will see God" (Matt. 5:8). If you want to see God do a miracle for you, then strive to have a pure heart. If you want complete deliverance from depression, stand before God with a heart ready to receive all that He has for you, a heart ready to be set free from a life of shameful acts.

Two Types of Sin

There are two types of sin in the life of the believer. Both are equal in the eyes of God and equally destructive to us. It is we who distinguish between the two. The good news is that both types are overcome by the work Jesus did on the cross—and setting us free of sin is God's favorite thing to do.

Now let's talk about these two types of sin. The first type is the sin that we hate to do but cannot seem to get rid of. These are the secret sins that bring with them great shame. We really do want to give them up, but we cannot seem to shake our unrelenting need for them. Often these are sins that no one needs to point out to us. We know it is wrong when we do them, for we often feel deep conviction from the Lord when we carry out our sinful desires. Even when we are in the act of these kinds of sins, we cannot fully enjoy our behavior, because true satisfaction can never be had in sin.

Habitual sin has ugly consequences. These consequences can be natural and outward, but often they are far worse when they affect our hearts. Psalm 106:43 says the people of Israel "wasted away in their sin." Many people feel this way when the sin they carry destroys their hearts. Carrying sin's heavy burden around is like carrying a purse full of trash. It serves only to burden us, not serve us. It smells so bad that we have to keep the purse zipped up, and it doesn't leave us any room to carry around the good stuff. The sin may be inside a really cute handbag, but it is still a bag of trash.

The apostle Paul talks about this kind of transgression in his writings: "For I have the desire to do what is good, but I cannot carry it out. For what I do is not the good I want to do; no, the evil I do not want to do—this I keep on doing.... When I want to do good, evil is right there with me. For in my inner being I delight in God's law; but I see another law at work in the members of my body, waging war against the law of my mind and making me a prisoner of the law of sin at work within my members. What a wretched man I am!" (Rom. 7:18–19, 21–24).

Of course, Paul was a holy man, filled with the Holy Spirit and completely committed to doing the will of God in his life. Yet even he struggled with sin during his time here on earth. We see in his writings that he wrestled with sin, hating his acts yet loving God. As Paul gave himself to the work of God, both acknowledging and confessing this sin, I have no doubt that God heard and answered his prayer by setting him free. When our sin becomes uncomfortable, it is a reminder for us to take it off.

The second types of sins are those sins that we still enjoy and therefore are not *willing* to give up. We even tell ourselves that this kind of sin is somehow OK, that God excuses it. These are sins we do willingly, despite knowing we shouldn't. Maybe we find our sin too unpleasant to relinquish. We tell ourselves, "Maybe the Lord will overlook this. I mean, He still loves me, doesn't He?" Yes, God still loves us, but His love for us does not diminish the repulsiveness of our sin to Him. As long as we follow Jesus, He will never stop asking us to give up and take off the garments of sin that weigh us down. King David calls this type of sin "willful sins." He writes, "Keep your servant also from willful sins; may they not rule over me. Then will I be blameless, innocent of great transgression" (Ps. 19:13).

Willful sin encompasses a great deal of our sinful behavior. It shows up when we think things such as, "I have a right to be angry over what he did." Maybe these kinds of sins seem so small compared to "big" sins that they seem silly to worry about. Or possibly these are things we think the Lord will overlook. "We need to live together before we get married—it is so common these days. Does it really bother God?" Even though this type of sin is called willful sin, sometimes it needs to be pointed out to us before we can see our actions for what they are. God's standards are somehow lost in today's liberal moral environment. These standards do not come naturally to any of us; they must be sought out and put into practice.

Because they do not come naturally and because the world does not practice these standards, how then do we know what pleases God? David tells us: "How can a young man keep his way pure? By living according to your word. I seek you with all my heart; do not let me stray from your commands. I have hidden your word in my heart that I might not sin against you" (Ps. 119:9-11).

The Lord has tucked His standards into His Word. By knowing the Word of God, we can know what pleases Him. As my husband and I have taught Bible studies to young singles, we have discovered that there are many newer Christians who simply do not know the Word of God. They may know the commands not to steal, lie, or murder, but they don't know God's standards concerning the walking out of our everyday lives.

It would be nice if ignorance somehow got us out from under the consequences of sin, but God's standard has been set since the beginning of time, and He changes not (Mal. 3:6). There is real comfort in that fact. God will never surprise us with new standards; we will never be left wondering what He is asking of us. This standard is written in the Word of God for us to plainly see, and God so loves us that He has written the standard into our heart as well (Rom. 2:15).

TAKING ACTION THAT LEADS TO FREEDOM

We must understand that freedom in Christ is tied to repentance. Throughout Scripture Jesus both healed *and* forgave people. It is also true that God only forgives us when we repent. And we repent only when we make a decision to *turn* from sin. Saying "I'm sorry" is not repentance. The Lord actually never asks us for an apology for our sin as people do. He is honored and worshipped when we not only acknowledge our sin but also turn from it. Actions really do speak louder than words when it comes to the kingdom of God.

Making things right with God is necessary, but it is also important to God that we make things right with other people. When we come to God to give an offering, Jesus told us what to do if our brother has something against us: "First go and be reconciled to your brother; then come and offer your gift" (Matt. 5:24). We may be suffering emotionally because we know something has not been made right between us and another person. In the Old Testament the Lord commanded the people that if they had harmed someone's property, they were to repent and then pay the person back at least double. Restitution is a biblical principle. If we need to go and make something right with someone we have hurt or harmed, now is the time to repent and to bring restitution where possible.

Repentance is also at the heart of all service to the Lord. We cannot come before God with clean hands until we have made amends for the wrong we have done either outwardly or within our hearts. And when we make things right with another person, we end up feeling better too. If you have past sin that has not been dealt with, the shame of it may be contributing to any depression you may be feeling. Many of the women I have counseled exhibit depression because of something that has happened in their past that remains unresolved today. Amazing freedom can be found by releasing these sins to the Lord.

One depressed young lady I met with suffered from extreme anxiety tied to a sinful event in her past. She could not move past the guilt and shame associated with this occurrence. She was too afraid to share with me what had happened, so I asked her to write it out on a piece of paper. Then, while tears streamed down her face, I asked her to repent, and then we burned the paper she had written on as a symbol of God's wiping away the sin completely. She felt so liberated after that and left my house a different person. Releasing sin does take the pressure off.

So why do so many Christians know God's standard yet still walk in their own way? Because we are very self-centered. In addition to that, many believers do not know *how* to break free from sin. We must have *power* from the Lord to break these holds on our lives. Good intentions are not enough. The Lord not only promises to remove our sin, but in His mercy He also promises to remove from us the guilt that results from our sin. Consider some more thoughts from David:

> Blessed is he whose transgressions are forgiven, whose sins are covered. Blessed is the man whose sin the Lord does not count against him and in whose spirit is no deceit. When I kept silent, my bones wasted away through my groaning all day long. For day and night your hand was heavy upon me; my strength was sapped as in the heat of summer. Selah. Then I acknowledged my sin to you and did not cover up my iniquity. I said, *"I will confess my transgressions to the Lord"*—and you *forgave the guilt of my sin.*
> —Psalm 32:1–5, emphasis added

If you are carrying guilt and shame from your past, it is time to let it all go and be set free. The Lord radically forgives us and tosses our sins into the ocean of forgetfulness. "As far as the east is from the west, so far has he removed our transgressions from us" (Ps. 103:12). People remember our transgressions, but God chooses not to.

Having our sin removed is like having layers of dust removed from our hearts. If you are serious about finding freedom from depression, then it is time to get the dust cloth out and go to work. When you release your sin, you will also release the shame and guilt you have been carrying and will free your heart to sing a new song. Let God restore purity in your life, and you will find the radical freedom you have been searching for.

Dig Deeper

1. What sins do you regret deeply but cannot seem to overcome?

2. What willful sins are you committing?

3. What do you think it means to repent?

4. What do you think about Romans 2:4, which says, "God's kindness leads you toward repentance"?

Assignments

The Lord caught King David in his adultery with Bathsheba and in having her husband killed in battle. The Lord used the prophet Nathan to confront David with his sin. Read Psalm 51, the prayer David wrote at this time in his life. Pray David's prayer earnestly for yourself.

Exercise 1: Take a moral inventory and release sin from your life.

"I will be careful to lead a blameless life—when will you come to me? I will walk in my house with a blameless heart. I will set before my eyes no vile thing" (Ps. 101:2–3). Ask the Lord to reveal to you any areas of sin in your life. In what areas of your life are you going your own way? Write these down.

Exercise 2: Pray for forgiveness for your sins.

"If we confess our sins, he is faithful and just and will forgive us our sins and purify us from all unrighteousness" (1 John 1:9). You must:

1. Confess your sins to the Father.

2. Ask Him to forgive you.

3. Ask Him for power from the Holy Spirit to overcome particular sins in your life.

4. Ask the Lord to remove the guilt of your sin.

Exercise 3: Ask yourself with whom you may need to reconcile.

Spend time in prayer and ask the Lord to reveal to you any person with whom you need to reconcile. Then write down that person's name (or people's names). If possible, contact that person and make amends. If it is not possible to contact the person, or if you know it would be unhealthy for you to do so, then speak forth your words to that person before God. Verbalize these words to the Lord as if you were speaking to that person.

Prayer time

Father, thank You that You stand ready to forgive me any time I come to You with a repentant heart. Reveal to me anything that is displeasing to You and that hinders me from following after Your ways. I release to You the sin of my past and ask that You erase my transgressions and wash me clean today. I desire to walk with You, and I am willing today to let go of anything that stands in my way. Forgive me, Lord, for sinning against You. Make me new and create a new heart inside me. In Jesus's name, amen.

Chapter 6

FORGIVE THOSE
WHO HAVE HURT YOU

*But you are a forgiving God, gracious and
compassionate, slow to anger and abounding in love.*
—Nehemiah 9:17

WHAT A FORGIVING and loving Father we serve! I love
the fact that God is both willing and able to forgive
us of all our sins, washing them away as we do a stain on our
hands. It is the finished work of Jesus that provides this permanent act of forgiveness by the Father for His children.

I have never actually been inside a jail cell (nor do I ever
plan on checking one out), but I was glued to the TV when
one of the educational channels did an exposé about what it
is like to be locked behind bars. The TV crew followed several
prisoners around for months in order to document their lives.
Only a few minutes into the program, of course, I was able
to see the potential for violence, gang-related activities, and
loneliness associated with life in prison. My first thought was
that there was no way I would want to go without makeup
and hair products for the length of any prison sentence! On a
serious note, though, that documentary scared me, and I felt
so blessed that I was watching it from my comfortable couch.

"Get Out of Jail Free"

Whether we know it or not, unforgiveness is really a jail sentence. By harboring unforgiveness and withholding grace from those who have trespassed against us, we unknowingly lock a piece of our hearts away. It is a myth that we gain power by withholding forgiveness, although we may feel powerful when we decide to withhold forgiveness from someone. But that feeling of power fades fast, and we are left with nothing but bitterness and sorrow at the end of the day.

Forgiveness is just like that "get out of jail free" card we all covet when we play Monopoly. Unforgiveness keeps us behind bars until one day we realize that the key to the jail cell, unlike that Monopoly card, has been in our pocket all along. The key that unlocks the door to our cell is simply forgiveness. Some of us harbor things in our hearts for months, even years. Just the name of the person who hurt us brings a sting. If that's you, then I offer to you a heavenly key that will set you free.

Whenever I minister to a woman suffering from emotional problems, I often start by asking her if there is someone she needs to forgive. It may seem strange that I don't begin with whatever her main issue seems to be, but I have discovered that forgiveness is a major factor in reaching spiritual breakthrough, especially in women suffering from depression. Unforgiveness literally rots the heart and is a major root of emotional torment.

Under the old covenant the priests of Israel would shed the blood of animals in sacrifice to the Lord, because "without the shedding of blood there is no forgiveness" (Heb. 9:22). Under the new covenant Jesus Himself provides the blood required for our sin sacrifice, and His blood not only cleanses us from our sin but also has the power to *cleanse our consciences* from acts that lead to death, so that we may serve the living God!" (Heb. 9:14, emphasis added). Jesus's blood was so perfect, so all-encompassing that it paid the price for *all* the sins of humankind, throughout all of history, and at the same time set us free from the shame that wrecks our conscience. And that's something to be glad about, because the removal of shame has a major part to play in a person's recovery. Shame does more harm to us than just about anything.

The exercises in the previous chapter prompted you to accept the covering of God's forgiveness and mercy over you and your life. I hope you were able to experience God's wave of forgiveness and cleansing through repentance. It is so wonderful to feel clean in the inner places of our hearts. There is no substitute for the peace that comes when we know that we are free from guilt.

Pay It Forward

We can never give to others what we have not experienced first ourselves. God has reached out and offered us forgiveness first—while we were still sinners—so that we would in turn have the power to forgive others. Sometimes our wounds run so deep that it *must* take God's power in us to truly forgive our enemies. In those cases forgiving others is not only an act of the will but also a work of the Holy Spirit. It is amazing that the Lord always makes the first move in our lives. It is His Spirit that first draws us to Himself. God first loved us so that we may love Him back. He was also the first to forgive our trespasses so that we may have a will and way to forgive others.

Every gift the Father has given us He asks that we stand ready to give away as we see other people's need for it. This goes for spiritual gifts as well as material ones. There is always a chain reaction happening in the kingdom of God: God gives to us so that we may give to others. God's kingdom works so completely backward from our human systems that it requires us to develop a new mind-set that is free from religious customs and worldly principles. The world says, "We wait to see what we can get from other people before we invest ourselves in them." The world says, "We only give when we can get in return." The world says, "Forgive only those you deem worthy of your forgiveness." The world's systems, however, will always distort what God has called us into as believers.

> You have heard that it was said, "Love your neighbor and hate your enemy." But I tell you: Love your enemies and pray for those who persecute you, that you may be sons of your Father in heaven. He causes his sun to rise on the evil and the good, and sends rain on the righteous and the unrighteous. If you love those who love you, what reward will you get? Are not even the tax collectors doing that? And if you greet only your brothers, what are you doing more than others? Do not even pagans do that? Be perfect, therefore, as your heavenly Father is perfect.
> —MATTHEW 5:43–48

We are challenged by Jesus to love those who are easy for us to love *and* those who seem impossible for us to love: "But I tell you who hear me: Love your enemies, do good to those who hate you, bless those who curse you, pray for those who mistreat you" (Luke 6:27–28). But we absolutely cannot love those whom we have not forgiven. We must first forgive and then make the great effort of loving those who have wronged us. Jesus told His disciples, "Freely you have received, freely give" (Matt. 10:8), as He sent them out for the first time. He was reminding them of the spiritual gifts He had give and asking them in turn to generously give these gifts to others. Forgiveness is a good gift to us from the Lord, and it is meant to be given away.

Forgiving Others Heals You

I have been told many times that forgiveness is for you, not the person you're forgiving. I can see why that statement has become so popular in our Christian culture, because in so many ways it is certainly true. People who have hurt us usually go on living life, completely unaware of the fact that we are suffering, while a part of us sits locked away behind bars as bitterness begins to take over. They are the ones who are in the wrong, yet they walk freely while we are left picking up the pieces of our hearts. How totally unfair. It is we who have been hurt who need the healing that forgiveness brings.

I have been left picking up the pieces many times in my adult life. I bet you have too. Maybe it is someone you loved who has hurt you the most. That happened to me when I was in my early twenties. I was devastated by betrayal, and at the time I thought I would never feel normal again. But God answered my prayers and lifted me out of the pit. Recently I again found myself hurt, this time by the actions of the person who was in my brother's life at the time of his untimely death. This person had damaged my brother's heart for years until it had been left completely broken.

Does the Lord expect us to forgive someone who commits the ultimate wrong against us? How do we possibly forgive under such circumstances? Jesus's disciple Peter asked the Lord the same questions. "Then Peter came to Jesus and asked, 'Lord, how many times shall I forgive my brother when he sins

95

against me? Up to seven times?' Jesus answered, 'I tell you, not seven times, but seventy-seven times'" (Matt. 18:21–22).

Jesus was telling Peter that we are to forgive as many times as we need to. For a time after my brother's death I woke up every morning and had to say within my heart that I forgave my brother's trespasser. The act of speaking out forgiveness over the trespasser's life was excruciatingly painful for me at first. Asking God to bless that person—I could barely let the words come out. Forgiving is not an easy process, especially if the offending person remains unrepentant and cruel. Our feelings scream, "I want justice!", yet the Lord says that He alone is our justice. Our feelings scream, "They don't deserve my forgiveness!", yet the Lord gently reminds us that He gave freely to us when we did not deserve mercy. Our feelings scream, "That person should suffer and see what he has caused me to feel!", yet the Spirit whispers to our hearts that Jesus died for that person too.

We may want the person who has hurt us to grovel in repentance, beg for forgiveness, and suffer deeply for his or her actions. But in my own journey of forgiveness the Lord has shown me that I must forgive without receiving from the other person any repentance, begging, or suffering. In fact, I must forgive even if throughout my entire life I never, ever hear, "I am sorry for what I did to your brother." Forgiveness is an act of the will, not a response based on our feelings. This is wonderful news, because it means that every one of us can forgive those who have hurt us—if we choose to do so. We do not have to wait to feel like forgiving the guilty party. If I always waited to forgive until I felt like it, I'm not so sure I would be a very forgiving person. I know I wouldn't.

Sometimes the saying "Time heals all wounds" is just not true. Some hurts are so deep, so lasting, that if we waited for the passing of time to mend them, we would never have the chance for reconciliation. When we choose to forgive, we can forgive those who offend us even if their behavior never changes—or gets worse. Our forgiveness is not based on their behavior but on our obedience to the Lord. Maybe that sounds familiar. The Lord chose forgiveness despite the behavior of those who offended Him—He gave His Son for our sin ransom long before we repented or even knew the Lord's call. Jesus's complete and perfect act on the cross was not dependent on our repentance but on the obedience of the Son to the Father.

We can forgive people regardless of their behavior, and that knowledge alone is very freeing. As our Lord hung on the cross, the Bible says that the chief priests, the teachers of the law, the elders, the governor's soldiers, and the criminals nailed beside Him all hurled insults at Him (Matt. 27:27–44). In the midst of it all we see our Lord making intercession for these people, asking forgiveness from the Father on their behalf: "When they came to the place called the Skull, there they crucified him.... Jesus said, 'Father, forgive them, for they do not know what they are doing'" (Luke 23:33–34).

Jesus purposefully said this prayer *out loud* from the cross so that His prayer would be recorded until the end of time. He meant for His words to be preserved so that we would model our lives after His example. Even on our worst day we must live in a perpetual state of forgiveness toward our enemies. No matter what anyone has done to us, the Holy Spirit can cause forgiveness to take root within our hearts. There is nothing anyone can do to us that the Lord cannot heal. God's power is above all things, superior to all our enemies. He has overcome all difficulties, including the unforgiveness we hold on to.

What is your story of hurt? Who has devastated your life by their words or actions? Whom have you still not forgiven?

Before you keep reading, write the names of these people down on a piece of scratch paper or on the margin of the page. Go ahead; grab a pen. And think about these names as you read on. The Lord is calling you to forgive these people.

LOOKING BENEATH THE SURFACE

"The good man brings good things out of the good stored up in his heart, and the evil man brings evil things out of the evil stored up in his heart. For out of the overflow of his heart his mouth speaks" (Luke 6:45). The truth is, as this verse makes clear, that anyone who has wounded you has probably done so because of a struggle going on inside them. Whatever people store in their hearts finds its way out of their mouths.

That's why that lady was so mean to you in the grocery line last week. She was having a miserable day because she was still angry with her sister from a fight they'd had the night before. That's why that bully in your kid's class is so cruel to your child. The kid is told at home that he is no good and never will be. That's why your boss is so verbally abusive. What you don't see is that his wife has just left him, and he is having a hard time holding it together. If the lady in the grocery line, the bully in your kid's homeroom class, or your abusive boss were at peace within their hearts, they would not behave badly. People whose hearts are at peace are patient, show kindness to others, and hold their tongues.

We do not have to war within ourselves because of upsetting outward circumstances. We must show grace and forgiveness to the people who hurt us, because that is how we are called to live in the kingdom of God. We can pray that those difficult people with whom we come into contact will find the peace they so desperately want. No one actually wants to live a life of unrest; turmoil is simply the consequence of sin giving birth in our lives. But King Jesus opens the door to peace, and the key to that door is the blood that He shed.

What do we owe the people who have wronged us? I learned more about the answer to this question and about my role in healing recently. I was praying with some friends on a hot and steamy summer afternoon several weeks after my brother died. They had come to pray with me through my grief and my struggle with forgiving the person who was in my brother's life at the time of his death. We settled down on the couch and began to pray. I was angry, grieving, and lost in my pain. Every single time the name of the person who had hurt my brother came up in conversation or in my mind, I felt physically ill.

Yes, I had said I wanted to forgive this person, but I didn't really want to—and I thought I couldn't do it. Some things seem almost unforgiveable, don't they? I had watched disturbing behavior by this person, and I was struggling with how to let things go. Before my friends came over that day, I had thought I'd already forgiven this person who had so hurt my brother in his final days, but after the counsel of my prayer partners, I realized that there were still remains of unforgiveness pulsing through my veins. That was proven by the fact that when I awoke each morning, I thought about this person. As I lay in bed at night I thought about the person's actions. I had become wrapped up in a blanket of blame. Although I was sitting in my basement with my friends, I realized then that I was in actuality alone in my own jail cell. I learned some things that day—and they launched me on my path to personal freedom through forgiveness.

We spend so much time trying to figure out why someone would want to hurt us or those we love. I spent a lot of time pondering this question following my brother's death. I looked for the reasons the person who hurt my brother had done certain things, why years had passed without a change of heart. Was this behavior caused by this individual's childhood, a sinful lifestyle, a heart full of hatred, or something altogether hidden? I made assumptions, placed blame, and stood in judgment of this person's actions. After all, the things the person had done were awful.

I thought perhaps I could forgive but still harbor an opinion about this individual. But my friend taught me a wonderful lesson on forgiveness that day as we prayed. She shared with me that forgiveness is only the first step toward healing. Then, after we forgive someone, we must choose not to put that person under judgment. In other words, we must stop making any assumptions about the person's character, standing with the Lord, or reasons for hurting us, and we must pass no more judgment. We cannot play God over anyone's life.

We must learn to allow the Lord to be our justice and the other person's judge. We cannot say, "He is evil," but must say instead, "He is hurting." We cannot bad-mouth that person to anyone, *most importantly to ourselves.* Once we claim to have forgiven, we must surrender our judgment over that person with both our *hearts* and our *mouths.* We can still be wounded, hurt, or even angry at the person's actions, but we must choose to show the individual who has hurt us grace.

FORGIVENESS HAS ITS REWARDS

Jesus said, "Do not judge, and you will not be judged. Do not condemn, and you will not be condemned. Forgive, and you will be forgiven. Give, and it will be given to you. A good measure, pressed down, shaken together and running over, will be poured into your lap. For with the measure you use, it will be measured to you" (Luke 6:37–38). This passage will challenge every religious bone in our bodies.

Let's look at a couple of very significant points from this scripture. "Give and it will be given to you. A good measure, pressed down, shaken together and running over, will be poured into your lap." Do you know that every time I have heard these words preached, it has been in relation to money? Maybe you have heard them presented the same way. I have heard countless ministers tell me that when I give into the kingdom of God, the things listed in the verse above are my reward. Perhaps they are well intentioned, but oh, how wrong they are. Let's reread this passage again, starting at the beginning. "Do not judge, and you will not be judged. Do not condemn, and you will not be condemned. Forgive, and you will be forgiven. Give, and it will be given to you."

This verse is in the context of the Lord teaching on having a heart of forgiveness rather than a judgmental spirit. What a revelation! This passage is talking about something much more precious than money. Jesus is saying that when we give unto others through forgiving and not judging, we will receive tremendous and limitless forgiveness from the Lord. Now that is a great reward!

Our level of forgiveness as well as our absence of judgment toward others matters very much to the Lord. He has placed such a high value on it that He gives us here an incentive to walk it out. Our incentive may not be counted in this life, but it will most assuredly be not only measured but also rewarded in the life to come.

Let's look at the last part of that passage. *"For with the measure you use, it will be measured to you."* You mean the Lord will withhold mercy from me if I withhold mercy from others? Surely not. Yet it is there and very clearly stated. As I studied this passage, I read the thoughts of John Wesley, the great eighteenth-century preacher, concerning this piece of Scripture. He said, "We ourselves are, as it were, to tell God how much mercy he shall show us!"[1] I have never heard this preached from a pastor. Usually we just hear sweet messages about forgiving our brothers and praying for those who have hurt us. All very important messages—but they leave out a most important doctrinal truth in the kingdom of God. *God measures the grace we extend to others so that He may measure us with the same amount.* Wow. Now that won't make most Sunday messages, will it?

Let's look a little further:

> "Forgive us our debts, as we also have forgiven our debtors..." For if you forgive men when they sin against you, your heavenly Father will also forgive you. *But if you do not forgive men their sins, your Father will not forgive your sins.*
> —Matthew 6:12, 14–15, emphasis added

Here it is again. Maybe God really does mean it. This time we see it tucked in at the very last portion of the Lord's Prayer, surely the most recited prayer of all time. Millions pray this prayer daily yet do not understand what they are asking of the Lord. In the Lord's Prayer we ask God to forgive us with the same measure of forgiveness we use toward others. This is quite a challenge from the Lord for us to start offering people radical mercy! As we learn to extend mercy to others, God will begin to bring healing to our own hearts.

As I studied the words of Jesus, I was compelled to change my thinking about people who are troubled or seemingly mean. Now I tell myself that these people are hurting, wounded, and need the Lord. God loves them as much as He loves me and as much as He loves my deceased brother. I pray for difficult people, asking the Lord to reveal Himself to them and to set them free from the trappings of this world. I had prayed these things before, but because I was standing in judgment on a particular person, I was never heartfelt in these prayers. By releasing my judgments to Jesus, I was able to begin saying these prayers and meaning them. The responsibility of the one who had hurt me in regard to my brother's death was now released into God's hands.

I found the key for getting out of jail, and I offer it to you. I know from experience that many depressed women have years of unforgiveness wreaking havoc within their souls. But forgiveness flips the switch and begins the process of inner healing in a way that nothing else has the power to do.

Let me be clear about the fact, however, that forgiveness does not always mean staying in a relationship with the person we are to forgive. Whether or not we are to remain in fellowship depends on the circumstances, and we must be led by the Holy Spirit in each situation. There are many times when the Lord will have us forgive someone, and He will show us at the same time that we are to break ties with that person. We must have a healthy life, and surrounding ourselves with a circle of close friends and family who are uplifting and not harmful is simply wise.

Sometimes the person we need to forgive is from deep in our past; maybe it is a parent who is no longer alive. Forgiving a person does not necessarily mean reopening our lives to them, particularly if the Lord asks us to close that door. Forgiving means forgiving, and that can be done a million miles away from the person we need to forgive. If you are living in a destructive pattern with a person, break fellowship with that individual. We can forgive people and yet keep ourselves from any wrong lifestyles they want to bring us into, choosing instead to follow the Lord and His teachings.

Two More Ways to Forgive

We tend to think forgiveness is only about forgiving those who have hurt us. But forgiveness does not stop there.

What about your self-inflicted hurts? Are there things you need to forgive *yourself* for? That question holds a great deal of weight, doesn't it? When we walk under an umbrella of unforgiveness toward ourselves, we are barred from receiving the raindrops of grace that the Lord rains down on us. Sometimes it is far easier to forgive others than to forgive ourselves. We live with constant reminders of some of our bad choices. What umbrella of unforgiveness have you been walking under?

You are worthy of forgiveness. It is amazing how many people live for years, even decades, with unforgiveness toward themselves, haunted by wrong decisions, broken relationships, harsh words, stupid actions, and the "I should haves" of life. Somehow the worst of our mistakes can plague us on a daily basis. Satan will remind us of these as long as we allow him to. But there is *nothing* that we cannot forgive ourselves for. *Nothing.* It is never too late with God.

"And we know that in *all things* God works for the good of those who love him, who have been called according to his purpose" (Rom. 8:28). *In all things.* That includes every mistake we have ever made, no matter the size. Every regret. *Regret* is a fancy word for placing blame in our own lap. Which things do you blame yourself for? Which regrets haunt you?

Regrets plague the mind and stifle grace. Now, it is important that we take responsibility for our past actions. Accountability and responsibility are useful in creating a right standard for living. But regret, shame, and unforgiveness are evil entities, meant to torture the mind and create the ultimate condemnation within the human heart. Forgive yourself and let go of regrets. Jesus paid the price so that we would no longer have to carry these things.

There is one more question to ask about forgiveness: Do you need to forgive God? I know, this idea may make you a little uncomfortable, but here's what I mean. God is perfect in being and power, holy in all His ways, yet He is blamed for a great many wrongdoings. We think, "God, You could have done...but You didn't." God gets blamed for world struggles, early deaths, sick babies, unresolved conflict, even destructive weather that we call acts of God. Is the Lord really to blame for the earth's sin and for Satan's evil works?

What have you blamed God for in your life? Do you hold a grudge against your heavenly Father? If you do, you must repent. God loves us, and it grieves Him when we place blame on Him. "For as high as the heavens are above the earth, so great is his love for those who fear him; as far as the east is from the west, so far has he removed our transgressions from us" (Ps. 103:11–12). He desires only good for His children, and He proved it by giving us His Son, Jesus, to save us from our sins.

Forgiveness is so very freeing. Forgiveness can do within us what nothing else can. It cuts us free of the ribbons that tie us to our yesteryears. The bottom line is that we really do need to forgive everyone who has hurt us, no matter how deep the wound. If you are serious about clipping the cords of depression that may be entangling you, then you will need to get serious about forgiving everyone in your life who has wronged you in the past or in the present. This is one step that we cannot avoid if we truly want to walk in complete freedom.

THE BEAUTY OF FORGIVENESS

A friend whom I'll call Amy was sexually abused by a close relative until she was thirteen. When she moved away from her abuser during her middle school years, she thought it was all over—including the mess going on within her. But a few years later Amy had to go to court about the abuse after a counselor alerted child welfare. Going to court must have been very difficult—it would have taken a great deal of courage for a child to sit and tell a judge such personal and disturbing details. Amy's mom wanted justice, but Amy just wanted it to be over.

The judge found the abuser not guilty, to everyone's surprise. Amy found out later that he had paid off the judge to ensure this verdict. Amy and her mother had no more money to fight with, so the abuser won.

As Amy shared with me the details of her life, I was so mad! How could the judge have done that! What a sorry excuse for a man of justice he was! But my friend was so at peace that she actually comforted me with her kind words.

Although Amy had been young when she was abused, she knew the Lord, and she had decided very early on to walk in forgiveness toward the man who abused her. But sometimes the Lord knows that there is more to draw out of us, a deeper healing that needs to unfold than we first thought was even possible. Amy shared with me that one day while she was attending a youth retreat, the Lord spoke to her about the matter and told her to forgive the man. Very tearfully she did. She said the words from the Lord that day were so clear they might as well have been audible.

Before that encounter with the Lord at camp, she said that she had prayed *at* God about the man who abused her. Now, after vocalizing her forgiveness for him in such a powerful way before the Lord, she realized for the first time that she could pray *for* the abuser and really mean it. "I never really understood forgiveness until then," she told me. "God actually gave me compassion for him at that point. This was a significant resource that helped me in everything God would call me to from then on."

But she had more to say. "Even though I believe my forgiveness was made complete at camp that day," Amy went on, "the Lord guided me into new levels of forgiveness in the coming years. He has given me instruction in this journey, showing me what I needed to do at each step." Several years after the youth retreat the Lord told Amy to call and to write to this man and convey her forgiveness to him. She didn't hear back from him after she sent the letter and left him a voice mail. Two more years passed, and by then Amy was in her early twenties. Yet again the voice of the Lord told Amy to contact the man to tell him that she forgave him. She called him, and after a decade of having had no communication, Amy was able to tell this relative that she forgave him.

Amy does not have a perfect relationship with this person now, but they talk, and there has been some restoration between them. Although the man is still not a Christian, Amy believes her act of obedience will pay eternal dividends one day. This relative once told Amy, "You of all people should not want anything to do with me." But Amy not only shared the gospel with him; by her actions she *lived* the gospel before him. "You are in total control of your own freedom when someone has wronged you," Amy says. "Forgiving the person is the easiest thing you ever do, although it is also the hardest. As soon as I forgave this man deeply, I was kicking myself, wishing that I had done it sooner."

Amy ended her story by stating two keys to forgiveness: first, forgiveness comes from the overflow of what God has given us. And second, forgiveness is all about us, not the other person. Amy radically forgave the man who abused her, and she forgave the judge who had withheld justice from her when she was a child. She now shares her story with others so that they too can find personal freedom through forgiveness.

Whom are you withholding forgiveness from? Are you ready to get out of jail? Make today your day of salvation (2 Cor. 6:2). If you are serious about becoming free from the grip that depression, fear, and anxiety may have on you, then one of the mightiest steps you can take is to walk in complete and total forgiveness toward everyone who has ever wronged you. Bravely release those who have hurt you so that you too may be freed.

Dig Deeper

1. Is there anything you need to forgive yourself for? If so, what?

2. Is there anything you need to forgive God for? If so, what?

3. How often do you pray for your enemies? If you don't pray for them, write down the name of at least one enemy and commit to pray for that person regularly.

4. Read the following passage: "For if you forgive men when they sin against you, your heavenly Father will also forgive you. But if you do not forgive men their sins, your Father will not forgive

your sins" (Matt. 6:14–15). What do you think of
this passage? Do you forgive others in the way
you want to be forgiven? Why or why not?

Assignments

Read this verse: "God is just: He will pay back trouble to
those who trouble you and give relief to you who are troubled,
and to us as well" (2 Thess. 1:6–7). When you are wronged, do
you think you need to seek justice, or should you let God seek
justice for you? Do you think God is just?

Exercise 1: Extend forgiveness to those who have wronged you.

- Make a list of people you need to forgive.

- Make a second list of people you need to stop
  standing in judgment over.

- Now pray over each person whose name you
  have written down.

Prayer time

*Father, I come to You now, and I forgive _____
for doing _____ to me. You have forgiven me
of much, and I choose to forgive _____ of
any harm that I have suffered. I ask now that You
give me a heart of love for this person. I pray that
You would reveal Yourself to this person and would
cause him/her to know You more. I do not stand in
judgment over _____ . I release this person
into Your hands. I believe that You are my justice,
Lord, and that You will take care of this situation.
Touch my heart so that I will not carry any wounds.
In Jesus's name, amen.*

Chapter 7

FIND YOUR
IDENTITY IN CHRIST

For in him we live and move and have our being.
—Acts 17:28

A NUMBER OF YEARS ago I went to buy a new cell phone
after I had moved to another state. I was all set to buy my
new phone until the salesman ran my name through the company's computer system. It was discovered that someone else
had gotten a cell phone through this national carrier using my
name and social security number. My identity had been stolen.
As many as ten million Americans a year have their identities
stolen,[1] a number that grows every year as more information
is made available to hackers through the Internet.

Our enemy, Satan, loves to steal identities. And unfortunately he is really good at it. He doesn't want Christians to
find out *who they really are*, because a Christian who has a
solid grasp of her identity in Christ is one powerful warrior
in the kingdom of God. Depression is one way the enemy will
absolutely steal a person's identity and in its place leave the
fingerprint of brokenness. But discovering our true identity
in the Lord will change everything. When we take back our
Christ-centered identity, we will conquer any stronghold that
depression or any other issue has on our lives.

A lot of Christians have their identities wrapped up in

something other than the Lord Himself. I say this with great love, however, because finding out who we are in Christ is not easy. For *every* believer, our identity in Jesus must be *fought for, sought after*, and *realized* every day of our lives.

WHO ARE WE, REALLY?

Our identity in the Lord is not something we are born knowing or can simply fall into. Finding our true identity only comes one way: by falling in love with Jesus. It comes by believing *His* thoughts about us above all others and *His* desires for us above all others. It comes by not only realizing His love but also by simmering in it all the time. There is no substitute for the presence of Jesus. It is His presence that changes our perspectives, lifts the veils from our eyes, and gives us clear vision.

To discover our true self (who we were destined to be by God), we have to dig, because often our identity is hidden under layers of self-doubt. This "Identity crisis" robs us of who we really are. Many people do not know enough about how God sees them, so they allow the world to tell them how smart or good or successful or important or pretty they are. Be mindful of the fact that someone is always waiting in the wings to tell you *who you are*. Are you going to believe them?

For some of us it is not the stranger who is the enemy; it is our own destructive self-talk. People who focus on negative thoughts allow their twisted perceptions and emotions to dictate everything in their lives. This is often how depression works as well. Negative emotions can hijack the senses, distort reality, and cast a dark shadow on every aspect of a person's life. When we are depressed, the way we see things is not necessarily how things truly are. Our senses can be very deceptive, especially when depression is in the driver's seat.

Our identity must be found in Jesus alone. Our sense of

111

who we are cannot come from our wealth, our spouse, our family, our popularity, or our education. We are to have eyes only for our beloved King Jesus, knowing that He looks upon us with undying love. He desires for us to be His bride, His betrothed. The problem is, many Christians have the engagement ring on, but few believers experience the glory and sweet security found only in knowing the groom.

It has always amazed me that adults can spend an entire lifetime trying to get over the events of their childhood. It would seem that a thousand years as an adult would not be able to compensate for those formative years. We learn so much about who we are early on in our lives. And sadly, many stand ready to receive their identity from any source but the Lord who created them. Every negative word spoken over our lives can alter our self-image. *Unless we allow God to remove those negative statements, we can remain crippled for a lifetime.*

Depressed people can often look back to a trigger that started the cascade. Perhaps it started with self-doubt, which began to overtake and then run wild—and then starved out the *real you.* We must learn to see with new eyes, to see ourselves as Jesus does: full of beauty, full of promise, a diamond in His kingdom.

Words certainly have a great deal of power. We are shaped by words—greatly shaped. Experiences shape us as well, but words set the trajectory. Satan uses negative events and the words that accompany them to change our perspectives about ourselves. Abuse along with the damaging words that accompany it is one of those things that always leads to an unhealthy view of self. We must identify the areas in which we have been affected and seek the Lord's touch to restore us to health in the Spirit. Satan knows that a wounded Christian is hindered in the kingdom of God. Release the wounds, and we release the church into the will of God.

We have talked about the power of forgiveness, but how do we cleanse the scars that are left in our lives once we have forgiven someone who has hurt us? Scars don't just leave when the person does. They must be dealt with too. Scars can have a tremendous effect on how we see ourselves. In order for us to have our identities firmly planted in the Lord, we must be free from the past. The past cannot define us—only the Word of God should have that place of authority. Jesus is our loving surgeon who speaks healing and truth to us through His Word, and He can completely remove our every wound and scar. God made us, and so it is *only* by the hand of the Creator that we can be healed.

The Lord alone should create our identity, because He loves us and created us. He alone knows our potential, since our potential waits like a seed within us As we grow in the Lord, our seed sprouts more and more, until like a tree, we have deep roots and rich fruit.

Who Is Shaping You?

"Yet, O Lord, you are our Father. We are the clay, you are the potter; we are all the work of your hand" (Isa. 64:8). We are indeed clay, and there is a potter at our wheel. We are always being shaped into some type of vessel, watered hands guiding our form. And although we are only the clay, we do get to appoint our potter—and unless we choose the Lord to be our potter, there will be other hands at work.

How do you see yourself, and whose words shaped the idea you have? The person who shaped the way you see yourself is the potter at your wheel. For most of us our life is directly tied to how others see us. But seeing ourselves through the eyes of others keeps us from discovering who we really are. Anytime we do not develop our own idea of ourselves, we unknowingly put our worth into someone else's hands. If we get approval from others, we feel good about ourselves, but if we don't find approval, we feel bad about who we are. This kind of teeter-tottering will leave us confused, and it will cause us to constantly doubt our value.

Many of you know that you need a new identity. The one you have is obviously not working so well for you. It is stained and shredded, marked up and abused. Maybe you have tried and tried to figuratively put that thing through the washing machine, even added strong bleach, only to have the same stains show through again and again. What you need to do is trash that old identity and get a whole new one—an identity not based on your past stains but on the perfect, blemish-free, perfectly white, new redemption of Jesus. "'Come now, let us reason together,' says the LORD. 'Though your sins are like scarlet, they shall be as white as snow; though they are red as crimson, they shall be like wool'" (Isa. 1:18).

What have you been told about yourself that you believed at face value? Maybe you were judged on your appearance. Or maybe you heard something like, "You'll never be anything." "You're not smart." "You're so ugly that no one will ever want you." "You're just a bad person." Or perhaps the words were a little more subtle: "You don't fit in." "You'll never be promoted." "You'll never make a better salary." "You can't go back to school." "You'll turn out just like your mother." Any of that sound familiar? Depression often causes us to replay these kinds of scenarios over and over in our minds, adding fuel to the fire. If we want to move on to healthier thought patterns, we have to shut off this recording.

It's true that every one of us in one way or another has an

orphaned heart, some scar from the past. The wonderful news is that while we may not have control over everything, we have total control over two things: first, *we choose whose words we believe.* And second, *we choose which potter guides our development.* These two choices shape everything else in our lives.

If we see ourselves through the eyes of our parents, our spouses, our enemies, our friends, our coworkers, or anyone else on the planet, then we are not seeing ourselves through the eyes of God, and we are failing to see what we can truly become. We can only wear one set of lenses at a time. When we choose to view ourselves through others' words rather than through the Word of the Lord, we stifle the great potter at His workbench. The only way for us to give back to God the control of the potter's wheel is to believe His Word above anyone else's.

We must choose to discount *everything* said or thought about us that does not line up with the Lord's thoughts about us. We must be willing to break away from every other perspective and accept only what the Lord says about who we are. God doesn't play games, and He doesn't manipulate us, disappoint us, or hold grudges against us. When we know the character of God, it becomes easier for us to release control to Him. Give Him the potter's wheel, and find your identity within His loving grasp.

HIDE YOURSELF IN GOD

We can find our identity in God only when we learn to hide ourselves in Jesus. Take a look at these two prayers by the psalmist:

> Let the morning bring me word of your unfailing love, for I have put my trust in you. Show me the way I should

go, for to you I lift up my soul. Rescue me from my enemies, O LORD, for *I hide myself in you.*
—PSALM 143:8–9, EMPHASIS ADDED

Keep me as the apple of your eye; *hide me in the shadow
of your wings.*
—PSALM 17:8, EMPHASIS ADDED

The character of God is wrapped in a million mysteries. He
is the God of thunder yet the God of rainbows. He shakes
the earth yet sends a gentle warm breeze. He is known as the
great I AM in a burning bush yet is flesh and bone in Jesus.
He reveals Himself in the shifting of seasons, in the making
of a butterfly, yet we must search out His voice in the stillness
of our hearts. He is the Lion and the Lamb. God is so big that
He has made the sun to rise and set on cue, yet He is mindful
of every need that we have (Matt. 6:8). He created the mountain ranges with His finger yet worries Himself to know the
number of hairs on our head (Luke 12:7). He directs the seasons with His breath and still bows close to listen to our secret
prayers.

The Lord knows when every bird falls from the sky (Luke
12:6) and notices each tear that falls from our eyes. He has
called each star by name (Ps. 147:4) and calls each of His children by name. He is a doting Father, no matter the number of
children He births. He loves in ways that seem strange to us.
He loves despite our wanderings. He is so grand, and we seem
so small. Yet in all His grandeur, God delights in revealing
His nature to us.

To accept what the Father says about us, we must first
accept the giver. The school of religion often has well-meaning
yet misinformed representatives. If we look to people to repre-
sent God to us, we can be easily disappointed. That is why we

must base our view both of ourselves and of the Lord on the Word of God.

Let's take a look at the nature of God as based in Scripture. As you read through these verses, ask yourself if you believe these truths for your own life.

God is good.

> But you, O LORD, are a compassionate and gracious God, slow to anger, abounding in love and faithfulness.
> —PSALM 86:15

> For as high as the heavens are above the earth, so great is his love for those who fear him.
> —PSALM 103:11

> Let them give thanks to the LORD for his unfailing love and his wonderful deeds for men.
> —PSALM 107:8

God loves you.

> Praise be to the LORD, for he showed his wonderful love to me when I was in a besieged city.
> —PSALM 31:21

> Though my father and mother forsake me, the LORD will receive me.
> —PSALM 27:10

> A father to the fatherless, a defender of widows, is God in his holy dwelling. God sets the lonely in families.
> —PSALM 68:5–6

> For as high as the heavens are above the earth, so great is his love for those who fear him; as far as the east is

from the west, so far has he removed our transgressions from us.

—PSALM 103:11–12

God hears you.

He fulfills the desires of those who fear him; he hears their cry and saves them.

—PSALM 145:19

God is a healer.

He heals the brokenhearted and binds up their wounds.

—PSALM 147:3

God is faithful.

The LORD is faithful to all his promises and loving toward all he has made.

—PSALM 145:13

God blesses people.

The LORD gives strength to his people; the LORD blesses his people with peace.

—PSALM 29:11

Do not be afraid, little flock, for your Father has been pleased to give you the kingdom.

—LUKE 12:32

God is close to you.

The LORD is close to the brokenhearted and saves those who are crushed in spirit.

—PSALM 34:18

God created you for a specific reason, and you have a mission and a purpose to figure out.

The LORD will fulfill [his purpose] for me; your love, O LORD, endures forever.

—PSALM 138:8

With this in mind, we constantly pray for you, that our God may count you worthy of his calling, and that by his power he may fulfill every good purpose of yours and every act prompted by your faith.

—2 THESSALONIANS 1:11

I cry out to God Most High, to God, who fulfills his purpose for me.

—PSALM 57:2

You are worth God's attention.

I have loved you with an everlasting love; I have drawn you with loving-kindness.

—JEREMIAH 31:3

God chose you from the beginning.

You did not choose me, but I chose you and appointed you to go and bear fruit—fruit that will last.

—JOHN 15:16

You are made by God to be holy.

But you are a chosen people, a royal priesthood, a holy nation, a people belonging to God, that you may declare the praises of him who called you out of darkness into his wonderful light.

—1 PETER 2:9

You are made in God's image.

Whoever sheds the blood of man, by man shall his blood
be shed; for in the image of God has God made man.

—GENESIS 9:6

God sees your potential.

See, I am doing a new thing! Now it springs up; do you
not perceive it? I am making a way in the desert and
streams in the wasteland.

—ISAIAH 43:19

GET SERIOUS ABOUT THE WORD!

I have not always had sure footing in this area of identity.
There was a time in which my identity was grounded in what
others thought of me, and I foolishly believed people's opinions about who I was.

During my college years I suffered great rejection from a lost
relationship. One person rejected me, and in my mind I may
as well have lost the whole wide world. Funny how my perception became so messed up because of just one lie that someone
told. Depression has the same tendency to blow a problem way
out of proportion. When we are depressed, one lie can develop
in us an entirely changed mind-set. One wound from the past
can fog our entire thought process.

I could have gone through the rest of my life feeling rejected
if I hadn't let Jesus tell me the truth. It really is sad that many
Christians carry around old hurts as if they were a badge of
honor and then use that badge as an excuse to be dysfunc-
tional. I don't know about you, but I hate dysfunction in the
body of Christ. I think it is time for the church to walk in
freedom. Let's throw those old badges in the fire, once and
for all.

The Word of God is amazing. It is alive and can infect every cell of our beings as we meditate on it. Chew on it. Let it take over your heart. Let it be the final authority in your life. Without the Word of God we will wander off on our own course, following our own mind-sets and beliefs. It takes daily application of and submission to the Word of God in our lives for its full effects to take over. I think that as Christians we can become frustrated when we "try God" and don't see the results we want. But we simply cannot think about God and His Word for only 5 minutes a day and expect that to combat the other 1,435 minutes of our day that are full of the world and its offerings. No, to get our minds, hearts, and self-talk to change courses and to move in the right direction, we have to become fanatics!

To find healing from depression, we must combat it with a total absorption in the Word of God. If we are trying to combat years of untruths, we cannot defeat them overnight. We must introduce the Word of God into our lives on a consistent, daily basis. Then we must be reminded of God's thoughts throughout the day by meditating on the Word and through prayer and fellowship. All day long? Yep. All day long you can realize God's truths about you.

When we think of prayer, most think of making our requests known before God (Phil. 4:4–7), but prayer encompasses so much more than that. The Bible tells us to "pray continually" (1 Thess. 5:17) or as the New King James Version puts it, to "pray without ceasing." Being in a state in which we acknowledge the Lord's presence brings us to His throne. Feel Him near; realize that He is beside you, even now. Throughout the day, thank Him for blessing you with that great parking spot, for the ability to hold your tongue around your coworker, for giving you peace all afternoon.

Tape Scripture verses around your home, in your car, and near your desk. Read them until they make a permanent home in your heart. Take time each day to read a devotional, to read Scripture, and to pray for your own and others' needs. All of this is prayer and can be done throughout the day, every day. Try it and see if you don't begin to experience God's beautiful presence building in your life.

The Lord's Word changes us. The more we welcome and incorporate His Word into our days and weeks, the more we will begin to change. If we want to see lasting change in our lives, it will require our time. We have to be diligent in keeping our identity, confidence, and security in God alone. Of course, God's view of us never changes; He always protects, always loves, always shows mercy. God changes not (Mal. 3:6).

Get to know the unchanging nature of God and His ways by studying His Word, because "the words of the LORD are flawless, like silver refined in a furnace of clay, purified seven times" (Ps. 12:6). Put on the lenses of the Spirit's truth, and see yourself through God's perspective. For in Him you will truly discover who you were created to become.

OVERWHELMED BY GOD'S LOVE

Sharon, one of the ladies who was part of my small group on being set free from depression, was literally stuck when we got to this chapter on finding our identity in Christ. She felt as if not one ounce of this truth was for her. God loved the world, of course, but surely He didn't love her, she thought. Sharon believed that God was angry with her, and her life, which was full of anxiety, reflected her belief.

One evening after I had taught the lesson, I asked all the ladies in the group to close their eyes and to imagine them-selves in heaven with Jesus. I asked them to talk with the Lord and to ask Jesus to take them to Father God. Many of the ladies in my group had never used their imaginations to connect with the Lord in this way, but I asked them to try anyway. I asked the ladies to have Jesus take them to the throne room of God, and then I asked them to crawl up into God's lap as if they were a child. As we prayed, I asked volunteers to tell the group what they were seeing and how they felt. The room filled with tears as these women experienced intimacy with God in a way they never had before.

Several months after this experience Sharon shared with me what had happened to her that evening. She had been totally set free from anxiety that night as she had experienced the love of God and realized that God did love *her* personally. Sharon told me how scared she had been to crawl into the lap of God, believing as she did that He was displeased with her. But she had asked Jesus to help her, and before she knew it, she pictured herself being placed right in the middle of the lap of God.

She said she felt as if she was a little child in her dad's lap, and a sudden rush of love filled her awareness. In that moment Sharon was overwhelmed by the love of God. She told me she was so changed by experiencing a new identity in Christ that the anxiety that had been such a part of her daily existence was totally broken from her life. She was completely set free, and only weeks after that night Sharon was ministering to other women who did not yet know their identity in Jesus. Amen! Maybe some of you need to crawl into the lap of God and experience His amazing, personal love. It will change your life and your identity.

Dig Deeper

1. In which unhealthy ways do you see yourself?

2. Whose words most shaped the idea you have of yourself?

3. What negative words have shaped you the most?

Assignments

Read Psalm 19:7–11 and Psalm 139. What does God see when He looks at you? How should you see yourself? How are you going to change your perception of yourself?

Exercise 1: Increase your intake of the Word of God.

"The law of the LORD is perfect, *reviving the soul*" (Ps. 19:7, emphasis added). No matter how young or old you are in the Lord, God is always looking to bring an increase of Himself into your life. In this assignment you are asked to increase the amount of time and energy you spend in God's Word. You get to choose the way you want to do this. Write down how you are going to daily draw closer to the Lord through His Word.

Exercise 2: Redefine your identity.

Make two lists. In your first list, write out any unhealthy thoughts you have about yourself. In the second list, write out how God sees you in the areas in which you see yourself negatively. Your feelings will try and convince you that your first list is the truth. As you write out your second list, ask the Lord to change the mind-set of your heart.

Prayer time

Spend time this week in prayer, asking the Lord to retrain your mind-set and identity.

Lord, I desire to find my security and my identity in You. Wash away all the old, unhealthy perceptions I have of myself and in their place deposit Your everlasting Word. Show me, Father, my value and my worth in You. I am a new creation in You today. Thank You that I am beautiful in Your eyes and greatly loved. Show me how to draw closer to You through your Holy Scripture. In Jesus's name, amen.

Chapter 8

CREATE A LIFESTYLE OF WORSHIP

I will extol the LORD at all times; his
praise will always be on my lips.
—*Psalm 34:1*

W HEN I ARRIVED at college, I totally adopted the lifestyle of a college kid. It has been a decade since I
graduated, but I still remember and miss the college experience. In case it has been a while since you were a student, here
are a few of the rules:

1. Don't schedule classes before ten in the morning.
   Only freshmen make the mistake of scheduling
   classes at eight o'clock.

2. Use your car to tell the world what you are into.
   I, for example, had my sorority emblem, my college sports-team stickers, and my Christian fish
   symbol all loudly and proudly displayed and
   hanging from various parts of my car. Can you
   say "tacky"?

3. Flip-flops are worn year-round. I would never
   do that now. What was I thinking?

4. Forget everything your parents taught you about
   cleanliness. I once lived in a dorm room that

had red mold growing on the tub, and I don't remember it bothering me that much.

5. The weekend starts on Thursday. Oh, how I wish corporate America would adopt this policy.

It is funny for me to think about that season of my life and how I totally adopted the lifestyle of a college student. I was in, 100 percent. I loved living with a million girls under one roof, eating out for three meals a day (if I did that now I would gain fifty pounds), and having more free time than I knew what to do with.

As disciples of Jesus, our lifestyle must be one of worship. When worship becomes our lifestyle, we will find that every aspect of our lives begins to exhibit this attitude.

One earmark of depression is forgetting to notice the blessings that surround us every day. Depression steals the song of our hearts and makes worship a difficult and taxing part of our Christian walk. Since depression kills joy, it can kill our worship to God as well. If we can learn to tap into the power of true worship to God, then the song of our hearts will change from despair to wonder. Worship ushers us into the presence of God, and the presence of God breaks the bondage of depression.

THE SWEET SOUND OF WORSHIP

What comes to your mind when you hear the word *worship*? Maybe old-fashioned hymns from your childhood church's choir. Or perhaps you have a more modern take on worship and imagine a worship band cranking out guitar songs with the lights turned down low and the words flashing by on the overhead screen. Maybe you see worship as the time you spend talking with God every now and again when you thank

Him for His goodness and for all the attributes that go along with being God of the universe. Maybe you think of the local Christian radio station that plays some really nice worship songs, especially on Sunday mornings as you make your way to church. Or perhaps you think of worship as something that happens only at church—the reverence of God made tangible.

If I asked one hundred people how each of them see worship, I would get one hundred answers. As fundamental as worship is to serving God, it is amazing how divisive a subject this can be for us. People actually get angry over this topic. *Churches split over this subject.* It seems that Satan would like nothing more than to keep the church distracted by tastes in music so as to divert the people from truly learning how to have a lifestyle of worship. Maybe you think that the fighting over worship styles is a new thing, only having formulated when the Christian rock band became a phenomenon, when youth groups started jumping for the Lord and raising their hands. You would be wrong.

Sadly, God's people have been fighting over the subject of worship since before Jesus came. We see this evident in the Gospels, which describe the very inflamed relationship between the Jews, who lived and worshipped in Jerusalem, and the Samaritans. Their squabble was due in part to the location in which they chose to worship God. The Samaritan people believed that Mount Gerizim in Samaria was God's holy mountain, and therefore they worshipped God there. Their Jewish neighbors believed that Jerusalem was where God was to be worshipped, and so they worshipped at the temple there. Jesus went out of His way to minister to the Samaritan people and even told a parable about the good Samaritan (Luke 10) to teach His disciples not to be hostile and discriminatory toward people who worshipped differently from themselves.

As Jesus neared the Samaritan villages, we can almost hear His disciples grumbling among themselves, saying, "Why in the world would He go there? Doesn't He know who these people are? They are the ones who worship God at Mount Gerizim." We hear the same tone from many Christians today: "Did you hear how loud that music was? Surely that's not worship." "They don't allow accompaniment in their church—don't they know that the Bible says to worship with instruments?" "Their choir only does old-fashioned music. Don't they understand that real worship means freedom?" I know you have heard it. You have probably even said it. I have. "Surely my way is better," we think.

If the heart of worship is to ultimately please the one being worshipped, we must discover how the Lord likes to be adored—and, conversely, to find out what displeases Him. Now the Lord's preferences have nothing to do with worship tastes, styles, or preferences. Actually, music selection is by far the least valuable element of what makes worship a sweet sound to the Lord. What matters to God is the heart of the one who is worshipping.

Although I have never heard the music in heaven, when I close my eyes, I can imagine that it is wonderful, amazing, made up of a choir of a million angels. But I cannot hum you its tune. That is why musical preference has so little value. When we sing or play, we are each simply trying to find a way to express our heartfelt love toward God. God made each of us so individually unique, both externally and internally, that surely He created people to worship Him in a thousand different styles and with tongues from every nation.

My husband and I have been involved for several years with missionary projects throughout Nigeria. We receive videos every so often of the work of the churches there so that we can see what our contributions have supported. One of the first videos I saw ended with the most beautiful worship I have ever seen or heard in my life. Surely it must have rivaled the angels' music in heaven. The village where the video was shot was filled with dirt huts that had leaves for roofs. The people wore secondhand rags, but they were more beautiful, more full of the Spirit of God than the members of any church I have visited in America. The amazing sounds of worship that flowed forth from these people's hearts as they played drums and danced in the warm night air were simply heavenly. Theirs was a language I had never heard, yet I knew what they were singing, and I knew what was in their hearts. The sounds burst forth straight from the worshippers' hearts and touched heaven.

Style has nothing to do with the heart of worship. Actually, music has very little to do with it either. King David, the greatest worship composer of all time, had only a little harp to play as he sang his songs of praise. The New Testament church, led by the apostles Peter and Paul, knew nothing of choir hymnals or soundboards. These early believers lifted up their voices in worship to God, and miracles came forth. One of the most amazing verses about worship is Psalm 22:3. It tells us that God inhabits, or is enthroned upon, the praises of His people. *God literally comes to dwell in the atmosphere of His people's praise.* What a miraculous promise! Depression tries its best to disconnect people from the heartbeat of God by stealing our thankfulness and our trust in God. If you struggle to connect with God in a real way, then begin by becoming a worshipper. There are guaranteed results.

Praise offered to God becomes a sweet aroma to Him, filling the heavens and delighting our Creator. We worship the God of eternity, the conductor of all who are alive and ever will live. This is how God describes Himself: "'I am the Alpha and the Omega,' says the Lord God, 'who is, and who was, and who is to come, the Almighty'" (Rev. 1:8). What a title. Who can compare?

The Lord has trillions and billions (I mean a lot!) of angels at His command, made and created to worship Him always and to do His will. Four cherubim angels, whose only job for eternity is to cry out in worship to the Lord Almighty, surround God's throne. "Day and night they never stop saying: 'Holy, holy, holy is the Lord God Almighty, who was, and is, and is to come'" (Rev. 4:8). God loves to be worshipped.

We Worship a Good God

It is much easier for us to worship our God when we are able to see Him for who He really is. Depression clouds our perception of the goodness of God in our lives. Spend time thinking about the God you are honoring. Picture Jesus in heaven, seated at the right hand of the Father. Picture yourself bowed down at the foot of the throne of God. Imagine the angels in heaven singing praises to the Lord's name. If you begin your time of praise with a heavenly mind-set, you will move into a state of worship more quickly. "Let everything that has breath praise the LORD" (Ps. 150:6).

God loves worship so much that He created us for it and made us to long for it. It is part of our very DNA, part of the way humankind was put together. In every deserted place, among every lost tribe, in every isolated region of the world, there is found a people who are worshippers. Even people who have never heard about Jesus worship something. Maybe they worship the sun, the harvest, or the trees, but worship is given by all of us, even without instruction or education. There is a longing within our hearts to tap into and recognize something greater than ourselves, and not only to recognize this greater power but also to actively engage in worship to it. It has been revealed through the Holy Spirit to believers in Christ that it is the Lord God Almighty and His Son Jesus alone who deserve our bended knee, our worship, and our wonder.

What is worship? How can something that seems so intangible be properly defined? *Worship is simply the expression of a grateful and thankful heart.* It takes place when the deepest place within us actively acknowledges God's mysterious attributes and His countless blessings. Worship is using what we have available to us to lift up in praise God's character—the essence of who He is. It is not merely a song but rather the expression of our devotion to Him. Worship is not music; it is action. Anything can be used to worship when it is offered to God with a heart of thankfulness. When we start seeing worship in these terms, we will discover that we have the ability to do a great deal of worship every day. Worship can become our lifestyle. *A thankful heart can follow us into every situation.*

We must also understand that God's worthiness to be adored has nothing to do with our view of what He has done for us. Let me give an example. After my brother died, I had a difficult time praising God. My worship fell silent. I felt hurt by God, feeling as if He had forgotten me. "God didn't come through," I thought. It seemed to me that there was nothing to thank the Lord for. In my spirit one day God asked me, "Am I not still God?" It was only my perception that had changed. Regardless of what had happened here on earth with my brother, God's majesty, greatness, power, and ability had not changed. God Himself was still the same, and He was still worthy of all my worship and devotion. My worship of Him could not be entangled with "What have You done for me?" thoughts.

God's goodness is not dependent on how He answers our prayers. His goodness was established before the foundation of time, and His mercies will reach through eternity. Worship should rise to the Lord not only when we are content and satisfied; real worship can also take flight on the winds of uncertainty, difficulty, and even pain. Honest worship soars because of God's unshakable attributes, lifted to God from our hearts by the wind of the Spirit. God has nothing to prove to us. *He is worthy simply because He is God.* Set aside any reasons that you may doubt the Father's love, and decide instead to focus on His eternal qualities that are unshakable. If depression has left your faith wavering, then cling to worship until your faith is restored.

TRUE WORSHIP: A SACRIFICE OF PRAISE

Satan tries to draw us away from worshipping God, and distraction is one of the means he uses. Isaiah 29:13 describes the attitude of people who have become distracted from God Himself: "These people come near to me with their mouth and honor me with their lips, *but their hearts are far from me.* Their worship of me is made up only of rules taught by men" (emphasis added).

The fact is, most Christians don't even need Satan's help in becoming distracted and heartless in worship. We tend to do a pretty good job of that ourselves by having a watered-down version of worship in our gatherings. Churches are full of people with unholy hearts who want to spend the fewest number of minutes in worship possible. These lukewarm believers look forward to the sermon so they can be blessed by a happy word before attempting to beat the crowds to Cracker Barrel. Those few minutes of singing at church is the only participation in worship they will have until the next Sunday rolls around.

Worship should never be considered a church performance or something we can miss in our hurry to get the kids to Sunday school before the preacher starts the sermon. A true worshipper of the living God will not be satisfied with fifteen minutes a week. A true worshipper fills every day expressing a thankful heart to God and relishes in time spent praising God's name.

The Lord wants us to be so filled with His Spirit that we cry out every day, "I will praise you, O LORD, with all my heart" (Ps. 9:1).

Worship is described in Romans 12:1 as a sacrifice. And as with any sacrifice, it must be given with a right heart in order for it to be accepted. Worship cannot be brought to the Lord as a means of gaining anything for ourselves. No, worship must be our time to give something to God. It is all about Him and His glory, not a time for us to focus on all the things we think we need.

One thing I know about worship is that it will always *require* something we have. It takes effort. It takes our undivided attention. It takes holy sacrifice. It has a value placed upon it from heaven. True worship always takes our focus off ourselves and our own needs and looks exclusively to God the Father and to His Son Jesus. *The heart of worship is not seeing what we can get from God but offering up what we can give to Him.* "God is spirit, and his worshipers must worship in spirit and in truth" (John 4:24). The Holy Spirit is responsible for *bringing* us into the presence of the Lord. Our worship will be dry, void of passion, and difficult to offer if we leave the Holy Spirit out of our efforts.

The Holy Spirit is the *breath* of God; He is the One who draws us to the Lord and fills us with Himself. Without Him worship music is just notes and words on a page. It is God's Spirit that makes us alive in our service to the Lord. Don't leave Him out. Philippians 3:3 says that we "worship by the Spirit." That means that without Him we are unable to come to God. Often the Lord speaks more to us during our times of worship than He does any other time. Or maybe it's that we *hear* Him better during times of worship, because our distractions are fewer.

There have been times when the Lord has spoken to me as I was cleaning the house or driving the car and asked me to spend time with Him in praise and worship. He has asked me to stop what I am doing and point my attention His way. I have found that if I obey this prompting, then 100 percent of the time I enjoy amazing moments of intimate worship with the Lord. Many of you may sometimes feel that tug on your heart, but you dismiss it quickly, not realizing that you have indeed heard the voice of God.

When we are sensitive to the Holy Spirit, He will direct us as to how to come into intimacy with Him. At home I have either my laptop or a worship CD that I can use to help me settle into a worshipful mind-set. In my car or when I am away from home, I have my iPod for playing praise music. The Holy Spirit knows when we need times of refreshing even before we do. When we worship, our very souls will begin to be filled with light, and the darkness of depression will begin to lift.

THE FRUIT OF WORSHIP

Let's take a few minutes to look at some fundamental truths about worship.

Worship refreshes the soul.

"The law of the LORD is perfect, reviving the soul" (Ps. 19:7). For a tree to flourish, sometimes dead portions of it must be trimmed away. Then new life can begin to sprout up again. A lifestyle of worship, of focusing on God's character and expressing the truth about who He is, restores the dead and dying areas in our lives. It provides water to our thirsty roots so that we can bloom in new ways. If we were to fully incorporate worship into our everyday lives, very soon we would start to see new growth forming in areas that seemed lifeless before.

Worship is not selfish.

"Jesus answered, 'It is written: "Worship the Lord your God and serve him only"'" (Luke 4:8). True worship points us away from ourselves and toward Jesus. Any worship born out of self-focus is unsatisfactory to God. For worship to be accepted by the Lord, our attention must be solely directed to Him as we bow at the feet of Jesus. Don't be fooled. The Lord will not accept the time we spend in halfhearted attempts at praise. He is a jealous God and does not want you to share your worship time with your to-do list, your self-centered thoughts, or anything else that makes Him second place. Set aside distractions and focus fully on the Lord, even if you have just a minute. We are *always* giving our time and attention over to something. If we do not deliberately give it to the Lord, then we will unknowingly give our best away to the world and not to God.

Worship is a choice.

"Give thanks in all circumstances, for this is God's will for you in Christ Jesus" (1 Thess. 5:18). Worship is not dependent upon circumstances. We see the heroes of the Bible often worshipping in the most tragic circumstances. The apostle Paul and his companion Silas worshipped in jail after they were severely flogged (Acts 16:23–25). Thankfulness and gladness can bubble out of us simply because of God's wonders, His awesome power, and His perfect holiness. Worship has nothing to do with our need for or even our dependence on Him, though we can certainly vocalize that to the Lord with joy. No, worship is not because of us—we worship God because of who He is, no matter the situation.

Worship comes from the overflow of a thankful heart.

"Give thanks to the LORD, for he is good; his love endures forever" (1 Chron. 16:34). No matter what has happened in our lives, blessings surround us. We need to take time to acknowledge and thank the Lord for our many gifts. I do almost all the cooking and cleaning at our home, and every once in a while after dinner, my husband will go out of his way to thank me.

I love the feeling I get when he shows me appreciation for the things I do for him and for our home every day. Our heavenly Father feels the same way when we express gratefulness to Him. What have you thanked Him for lately?

Worship touches heaven and pleases God.

"Enter his gates with thanksgiving and his courts with praise; give thanks to him and praise his name" (Ps. 100:4). God will always give His ear to a man or woman who worships Him. Thanksgiving and praise draw us into the presence of the Lord. Worship is a surrender of our time, attention, and thoughts to Jesus.

Worship changes our perspective.

"Blessed are those who have learned to acclaim you, who walk in the light of your presence, O LORD" (Ps. 89:15). Worship makes God bigger and our problems smaller. Knowing and acknowledging that we serve a huge God puts our difficulties into perspective. The biggest need in a depressed person's life is for a new perspective, a new outlook, and new way to view life's tough circumstances. In many cases our circumstances may not change. Our kids may continue to act up, our husbands may not learn to appreciate us, our pay may not reflect our hard work, and our bodies may not be healed. When circumstances stay the same, the only thing that can change for the better is our perspective.

Worship establishes the kingdom of God in our lives.

"The kingdom of God does not come with your careful observation…because the kingdom of God is *within* you" (Luke 17:20–21, emphasis added). Worship brings our hearts and minds into a right state. As believers, we must strive to usher the kingdom of God into the earth. This starts in our hearts. For the kingdom of God to come forth within us, we must be properly grounded in the Word of God. Baby Christians need others to feed them the Word of God. As we grow to maturity in Christ, we need to take hold of and devour the Word on our own. Once the Word of God is sown in our hearts, worship is what waters the seeds.

Worship invites the Holy Spirit into our life.

"Yet a time is coming and has now come when the true worshipers will worship the Father in spirit and truth, for they are the kind of worshipers the Father seeks" (John 4:23). I once heard that reading the Word of God is like breathing in deeply of the things of the Spirit and then breathing out the contaminants of the world. Worship, similarly, is like taking a big sip of cool water for our souls. Just as the Word flushes out the mind-set of the flesh and counteracts the messages of the world, so too does worship. It causes an exchange to take place. We exalt the Lord and give Him our worries; He in turn fills us with His Spirit and reveals to us His presence. Now that is a pretty wonderful swap.

Worship breaks strongholds in our life.

"And whenever the tormenting spirit from God troubled Saul, David would play the harp. Then Saul would feel better, and the tormenting spirit would go away" (1 Sam. 16:23, NLT). God's people are set free in His presence. During times of worship, the Lord will often usher in His healing. For example, when King Saul was tormented by an evil spirit, David was asked to come and play worship songs on his harp for the king. The presence of God would fill the room, and the evil spirit would leave. "You will fill me with joy in your presence" (Ps. 16:11).

When you are suffering from depression, fill your life with worship. A family member of mine was going through a very traumatic divorce and was filled with depression and anxiety.

She began to carry worship music with her wherever she went in a little tape player. She played it in the background when she worked, when she was at home, and when she had trouble falling asleep. Just as King Saul had, she found that she felt better as she was soaked in praise music. The presence of Jesus always ushers out the presence of darkness. When we find ourselves in really dark places, the best thing we can do is bathe our atmosphere in worship. When you find that you cannot pray, turn on music that invites the Holy Spirit. "Come, let us bow down in worship, let us kneel before the LORD our Maker" (Ps. 95:6).

Worship is very helpful, especially for those who suffer from extreme anxiety. I have found this to be the case with many of the women I have ministered to. When nothing else seems to work, playing worship music has the greatest results. If you struggle when you are at home by yourself or late at night when you need to go to sleep, try playing worship music that is soft and melodic. Anxiety for many people is a difficult part of the struggle with depression. It robs us of our contentment and our ability to sit still and enjoy life. If you battle anxiety, try making worship music a daily part of your recovery.

Dig Deeper

1. Before you read this chapter, what did you think worship was?

2. Now that you have read the chapter, how do you view worship?

3. What holds you back from worshipping the Lord more than you currently do?

4. What are some different actions that can become worship?

Assignments

Read Psalm 63:1–6 and Revelation 4:1–11. Describe the throne room of the Lord.

Exercise 1: Intensify worship in your life on a daily basis.

Decide how you are going to make worship a priority in your life every day, and write down your ideas. Maybe you can start your morning by listening to praise music instead of watching the news. Or you might want to listen to praise and worship music in your car on your way to work. You might decide to listen to worship as you work out. Intensifying worship in your life will be a blessing. Give it two months and see if you do not notice a change in your outlook. When you have a really bad day, turn your praise music on. Remember, God inhabits the praises of His people (Ps. 22:3).

Exercise 2: Arm yourself with music that will lead you into a mind-set of worship and praise.

If you do not have a great go-to collection of CDs that will help you enter into worship, it is time to invest in some tunes. Load up your iPod, your laptop, and your car with worship music. I search out YouTube and listen to great music for free all the time. A recent style of music that has become popular for worship is called "soaking music." The term *soaking* simply refers to spending time basking in God's love and grace. Do searches for "soaking worship music" online, and you will find a wealth of music to help you enter into praise and worship unto the Lord.

Exercise 3: Count your blessings.

"Blessings crown the head of the righteous" (Prov. 10:6). Blessings surround each of us, even when we do not feel as if they do. Make a list of your blessings from the Lord. After you have made your list, thank the Lord for all that He has given you.

Prayer time

Spend time listening to praise and worship music. As your heart enters into worship, spend time in prayer telling the Lord of His goodness, His wonderful attributes, and His glory. Thank God for each blessing you have in your life. Instead of asking the Lord to answer your prayers, focus completely on giving praise to God.

Lord, You are doing such amazing things in my life every day. Thank You for loving me and for sending Your Son, Jesus, to rescue me. You are magnificent and mighty. You are worthy of all of my praise because of who You are. It is an honor to worship You with my life, my words, my deeds, my money, and my very breath. My desire is to bring You honor and worship in every area of my life so that Your glory will be seen through me. Make me a true worshipper, with a heart that is pure and full of Your love. Allow me to experience Your presence more and more each day so that I can fellowship with You in ways I never have before. You are my greatest gift, and to worship You is my greatest privilege. Amen.

Chapter 9

SEEK GOD'S WILL

I cry out to God Most High, to God, who
fulfills his purpose for me.
—*Psalm 57:2*

FOURTEEN YEARS AGO the Lord revealed to me in a dream the man I would one day marry. Four years later I met this man from my dreams. At the time of the dream, however, I was a broken girl with terrible insecurities and crippling anxiety, desperately praying to God for a husband. In the dream I saw a kind man with short, dark-brown hair smiling at me. More than anything about the dream, I remembered the way this man made me feel: secure, loved, and content. I remembered the kindness of his smile. The dream felt so totally real that I woke up the next morning and was compelled to write down what I had experienced.

The face in the dream faded, but the imprint of my meeting with that man never left my heart. At the time of the dream I was drawn to guitar-playing, long-haired, worship-leader type guys, so I almost dismissed the short hair of the man in my dream, thinking God had made a mistake. Well, God was right on the money. I am now married to Kevin, who matched my dream exactly. He keeps his dark brown hair trimmed short, wears a polo shirt every day, and cannot carry a tune or play an instrument. I thought I knew the kind of man I needed, but the Lord had a better plan. And the way I felt in the dream is how Kevin makes me feel every day: secure, loved, and content.

The Lord has spoken to me only a handful of times through dreams. But every time He has, the Lord has opened heaven and given me a glimpse into His plan for my life. I wish I could get this kind of direction on a weekly basis! But this kind of extraordinary blessing comes only at appointed times. Each dream I've received from the Lord has brought me direction, confirmation, or a specific message. And as I've looked at the larger picture, these divine gifts of communication have convinced me that the Lord is very involved in shaping our destinies and stands ready to draw each of us into His will for our lives. Sometimes God "lifts the veil" of our futures and reveals to us a piece of His divine puzzle through dreams and visions, but more often He speaks to us in subtle ways, gently pulling us toward our destiny in Christ with each new directive.

SEEING THROUGH GOD'S EYES

For a while we've been talking about letting go of things that move us in a wrong direction. Now let's begin looking at how we can move toward our *right* direction, or God's will for our lives. To do this, we must start seeing the things around us through the eyes of the Holy Spirit.

I have a degree in microbiology, and everything I learned in science taught me to rely only on what can be absolutely proven through observation and evidence. So many of us approach our lives as a scientific study, only believing in the things we can detect through our five senses. Most people believe that we are simply natural beings looking for a spiritual connection with God, but we are really spiritual beings who happen to be in a natural body. If we focus on human observation alone, any depression we have may get even worse. We must learn to see and hear by Spirit of God and not just through our natural senses.

When we make judgments based only upon what we observe in the natural world, we are limited to tunnel vision, seeing solely the things that are right in front of us. God, however, has the longer view, the higher perspective that cannot be detected by our natural senses. He sees in every direction, not only in this life but also for our eternity as well. For us to properly judge the purpose of our lives, we must tap into God's bigger plan for us. Only then will we unwrap our significance and our purpose.

Real significance can be found only through the Lord, because a life filled with meaning affects not only our time in this world but also our future in the world to come. If you feel disappointed and depressed and believe that your life is pointless, stop laboring in vain for the things of this world. You need to labor instead *in* Jesus and *for* Jesus. Only then will you begin to operate with an eternal perspective, which is a priceless asset in this life, and find your true purpose. My favorite Bible teacher, David Pawson, quotes his father as saying, "Life is long enough to live out God's purpose, but it's too short to waste a moment."[1] So let's get busy finding out what God's will is for our lives.

To do that we must begin by being filled with God's desires, by wanting His will above our own. I have often found myself praying for God's plan, but deep inside all I really wanted was my own. Too often Christians offer up their plans to God and then ask Him to bless the plan. Or we create conditions under which we will follow Him. A mature believer knows that we cannot follow God while clinging to our own premade plans or lists of conditions. It sounds nice to tack "let Thy will be done" onto the end of a prayer, but simply using that phrase can't cover up selfish motives.

There can be a great divide between our plans and God's will. If our plans are not merged with God's, our faith can be destroyed. God's will can be so different from ours. His perfect timing can seem to be our worst timing. God's will can feel downright painful to our flesh. But we know that outside of God's will, things will never come together correctly. In contrast, when we discover the perfect will of the Father, we are energized by a power larger than ourselves, and we see miracles unfold before us. It is imperative that you and I find out what God's plans for us are and that we join in the adventure of faith.

As we stand before God waiting for our complete inner healing from depression to take place, we must realize that the only way to arrive at wholeness is through the door of the Father's will. It is a door that will change our lives, maximize our gifts, and bring significance to our souls. It is also a door that may challenge everything we know about God and require us to give up any dreams that are outside God's will or timing. But stepping through the door of God's will is so worth it in the end.

Let's take another look at Psalm 57:2, the verse at the beginning of this chapter: "I cry out to God Most High, to God, who fulfills his purpose for me." I became obsessed with this scripture during a period of time when I was confused by the direction in which my life was going. I learned that it's up to God to guide me into my purpose. That fact sure takes the pressure off us, especially when we feel as if we are moving at a hundred miles an hour—and no one seems to be driving the car! But the Lord is there, even when we cannot see Him. He has each path, each turn, and every stop mapped out for us, even when we are convinced that we have gotten totally lost. Moving toward God's plan for our lives will lift the veil of depression and establish a purpose for our steps.

One Sunday night as we taught one of our Bible studies, my husband and I asked each person in the group to come to us for individual prayer. Before we began praying, we asked each person what he needed from the Lord. We were completely surprised to find that almost every individual in the room said the same thing: "I want to know what God's will is for my life," or, "I need God's direction." Isn't that what every follower of Jesus wants to know? That is why Rick Warren's book *The Purpose-Driven Life* made the best-seller list. We all want to know why we are here; we all want to be given our heavenly assignment and see it fulfilled in our lifetime.

The truth is, we will forever be searching out God's purposes for our lives, because with each fulfilled season, there is another season of life ahead waiting to be discovered. To put in another way, once we move into position in our current assignments, God then starts preparing us for the next task. As we follow the Lord, He propels us forward through His Spirit, on and on from one glorious assignment to another. We will never quite *arrive* until we meet the Lord one day. Many of my single girlfriends are always longing for that "someday" when they find Mr. Right, and they sometimes miss the assignments in the season of singleness in which they currently live. We all have a tendency do that—to hurry along to the next big thing. Could we be missing *today* because our eyes are only on *tomorrow?*

One thing to keep in mind is that *each day* we can be fulfilling our purpose in Jesus as the Lord gently pulls us toward His larger plan for our lives. Sometimes this slow pace can make us feel as if it will take forever for us to reach our next destination. I know how that feels. It feels as if it will be forever until my husband and I start a family, forever until our business gets off the ground, forever until we reach the ministry that is within our hearts. I am always waiting for the next assignment. What are you waiting on?

WAITING CAN BE TOUGH

The Lord can surprise us and be the God of the "suddenly" when we least expect it, but most often the Lord seems to take His time, using the day-by-day moments to draw out of us the impurities we don't even know are there. Frequently the Lord's will for us requires a time of waiting. We want fast-food drive-through service, but the Lord often serves us from a slow cooker. The waiting, though painful, can be used by the Master to paint His masterpiece within our hearts. Ephesians 2:10 says, "For we are God's workmanship, created in Christ Jesus to do good works, which God prepared in advance for us to do." We are all undergoing construction by the master carpenter so that we may fulfill the plans and purposes God has already chosen for us.

Jesus was described as a "man of sorrows, and familiar with suffering" (Isa. 53:3). Romans 5:3–4 tells us to "rejoice in our sufferings, because we know that suffering produces perseverance; perseverance, character; and character, hope." Every great man or woman in the Bible walked through some type of suffering as they walked out God's plan for their lives.

Suffering. I used to cringe almost every time I read a scripture about suffering. I was more confused than anything. I really struggled with why God would allow suffering for His people. Now that I am growing older and have passed through the valley of suffering several times in my life, I can stand at a vantage point atop the mountain and look back on the journey I have made with new eyes.

Suffering produced a fruit in me that never would have been birthed in any other way. This fruit is sacred to me, because it was born out of many tears and a broken spirit. It is fruit that is beautiful to Jesus, because He knows the pain in which it was ripened. God's will may lead you through a season of suffering. It hurts to let go of old habits, unhealthy relationships, impure attitudes, lusts of the flesh, and abusive behavior. Suffering could also mean letting go of your own dreams, your need to control, your judgmental heart, or your tendency to gossip. Trials too bring their own form of suffering. No matter the source, suffering can change us on the inside in a way that makes us stronger men and women of faith.

"In this you greatly rejoice, though now for a little while you may have had to suffer grief in all kinds of trials. These have come so that your faith...may be proved genuine and may result in praise, glory and honor" (1 Pet. 1:6–7). The Lord's first priority is not necessarily our comfort. He is much more concerned with the temperature of our hearts. Trials and suffering can actually move us more quickly toward God's will than just about anything else, because during times of pain we see our need for Jesus more clearly and become more dependent upon God than at other times. When I was walking in the valley of suffering, every step felt impossible, and giving up seemed like a real option for me at times. The pain exposed my weaknesses and made me turn my face to the Lord all day long. Literally all day long I surrounded myself with the promises in God's Word, and I cried out to God for help.

The darkness of depression will either make us fall at the feet of Jesus and ask for His mercy to come upon us, or it will cause us to turn away from God's love, blaming the Lord as we walk away. I have watched these two choices play out in countless lives, my own included. If you have not yet come to the Lord admitting your weaknesses and your need for Him, come to Him now and stay by His side.

Jesus goes before us to make our paths straight. The path for each of us is not a perfect road without hardship, but Jesus goes before us to map out our destinies. Some of you may feel as if you are walking on your path without the help of the Lord. You may have stubbed your toe and fallen a few times along the trail, and now you doubt if God is even walking beside you at all. But even though depression has masked the Lord's presence in your life, your hand is tightly held in His, and He is walking you toward your healing. His presence is not dependent upon our ability to sense Him near us. Jesus is near, regardless of how we feel or what we see.

LEARNING TO HEAR GOD'S LEADING

Satan can use events in our lives to change our perspective and to get us off our path. But if we seek God, *these events will not be allowed to change our destinies.* God appointed our destinies long ago, and if we follow the Lord, not even Satan can derail God's plans for our lives. I love knowing that in the middle of my wandering in circles, God is in control and will see me through.

God does give us the ability to walk away from our destinies and purpose if we so choose. The Bible is full of true-life tales of people who missed the mark and walked outside the will of God for their lives. I think of Samson, the handsome hero of the Book of Judges who was born with the gift of great strength from the Lord. Through unwise decisions Samson was blinded, imprisoned, and made to grind grain until he died by pulling a Philistine temple down upon himself and upon the Philistines with him. Not exactly the happy ending he could have had if he had obeyed the Lord.

I am reminded too of King Solomon, the richest and wisest man ever to walk the earth. Solomon was led astray when he took pagan women to be his wives and then began to worship their gods. God was so disappointed in him that He punished Solomon by tearing his kingdom in two after his death. You can read his story in 1 Kings. Samson and Solomon were gifted, anointed men, poised to be leaders in their lifetimes. But each of them was led astray by his own desires.

In the New Testament we see the Pharisees refusing to follow God's plan. "All the people, even the tax collectors, when they heard Jesus' words, acknowledged that God's way was right, because they had been baptized by John. But the Pharisees and experts in the law *rejected God's purpose for themselves*" (Luke 7:29–30, emphasis added). If the Pharisees had been able to hear the voice of God, they would not have dismissed Jesus as the Messiah. We must be careful not to reject or despise the plan that the Lord has for us when His will doesn't line up with our own plans. Walking with the Lord means being flexible to move when the Lord tells us to move and letting go of any dreams that do not bring us closer to God's plans for us. How do we find out God's will for our lives? We discover it by prayer. *Prayer aligns our will with God's.* When we need direction, we must go to God. In addition to praying, it is very important that we learn how to hear God's answer so that we may know His will. *As we walk toward healing from depression, it is imperative that we hear directly from God so that we will know how to adjust our lives, our time, our decisions, our relationships, and our prayers and be able to press on toward wholeness.*

Prayer is a continuous conversation with the Lord in which

we talk but also listen. If we are seeking a specific answer for a situation, we are to bring our request before the Lord and then, after asking our question, wait. The Lord may give us peace toward a yes, tell us no, or show us that we need to wait. The good news is that it is actually quite easy to begin to hear from God for ourselves. Not only do we have the Word of God, which communicates God's direction to us, but we also have the Holy Spirit who stands by, ready to speak with us.

The Lord is the God of peace, and His Holy Spirit speaks to us through what I call our "peace barometer." When we feel unsettled about something in our hearts, *no matter how good that thing may look at the time,* we know that we should not move toward it. Anytime we consider a situation and realize that we feel unsettled, that we lack peace in our spirits about it, please know that this is the Holy Spirit *telling us to not go forward!*

So many women have told me, "You know, at the time I didn't have any peace about doing that, but I did it anyway." Only after I taught them the "peace test" did they realize that they had actually heard the voice of God and just hadn't realized it. So many things may look good when we first consider them, yet down the road they turn out not to be beneficial. The Holy Spirit knows what is to come, so we must learn to follow Him and choose not to look to the world to guide us. It takes practice to hear from God, so begin asking Him questions, and believe that He will answer you. Practice the "peace test" as you make decisions. When you are at a crossroads, simply pray, and ask yourself, "Which option do I feel more peace about?" The more often we tune our ear to God's channel, the easier it will be for us to hear His voice.

Psalm 40:8 says, "I desire to do your will, O my God; your law is within my heart." When we have the Word of God in our hearts, it will produce a godly desire. If our desires are all over the place and lack a godly focus, then the solution for us is to get deeply entrenched in the Word of God. God's Word will give us wisdom, and wisdom will guide us into God's perfect will.

I thought I was going to be a doctor, and I studied through college with the dream of treating patients one day. When medical school did not work out for me, I was devastated. Now I had nothing but a dead dream and no idea what lay ahead for me in the future. The Lord opened doors for me in another area, and now I am *so thankful* that God did not answer my prayer regarding my desires to be a doctor. He knew better. If I had continued on to medical school, I am convinced that I would have walked away from the real plan God had mapped out for me.

God gave us His Holy Spirit to be our Counselor—to be our spiritual compass when we need direction. The psalmist knew that; he wrote, "You guide me with your counsel" (Ps. 73:24). It is very easy for us to run to friends, a spouse, or other family members when we need direction concerning a situation. And although others' opinions can help us, *we must ultimately learn to hear from God ourselves and not depend on other people to make choices for us.*

I have a friend who allowed her parents to make major decisions for her, even after she became an adult. The result was that she was not always happy with the outcomes of her parents' choices, because she depended on their answers more than on God's. It is a difficult cycle to break if we have developed the habit of needing other people's approval before we make decisions. But God's counsel and direction for us will always be in perfect alignment with His will.

The Lord made us a powerful promise in Isaiah 30:21. He

said, "Whether you turn to the right or to the left, your ears will hear a voice behind you, saying, 'This is the way; walk in it.'" It is a glorious promise that the Lord Himself will speak to our spiritual ears and give us certain direction. No matter where we find ourselves in life, the Lord will reveal His will to His children. How do we have such a relationship with the Lord that we are in a position to hear His voice? His invitation is only for the thirsty.

"Come, all you who are thirsty, come to the waters; and you who have no money, come, buy and eat!" (Isa. 55:1). God's currency is a thirsty heart, a heart that longs for righteousness. Only the thirsty find God's perfect will. As you seek healing for depression, realize that a thirsty heart will be quenched. If you focus on thirsting after God, the Lord will establish Himself and His rewards inside you. Expect to hear from God. I never read the Bible, write, or pray without the expectation of hearing directly from the Lord. Many Christians have no expectation that the Lord will speak to them, and silence is surely what they experience. God wants to reveal His will to you. Jesus said, "Your Father has been pleased to give you the kingdom" (Luke 12:32).

God's Will Is Good

As we search out our specific call in Christ, it is God's will to do good things in our lives. Let's look at some fundamental principles that apply to anyone who is pressing toward emotional healing.

It is God's will to bring us restoration.

"And the God of all grace, who called you to his eternal glory in Christ, after you have suffered a little while, *will himself restore you and make you strong, firm and steadfast*"

(1 Pet. 5:10, emphasis added). I lived off 1 Peter 5:10 when I was searching for healing from depression. It became a personal promise to me, as if Jesus had written these words for me alone and slipped them under my pillow. I had this verse memorized, and I said it to myself every day, all day long if I needed to. I felt that restoration was near, and I used this verse to hold me until that day of deliverance came. I can say today that I am strong, firm, and steadfast, just as God promised me.

You must know that God's will for you is restoration. His desire is that you "forget the shame of your youth" (Isa. 54:4). The Lord is an expert at restoration. He restored Moses and Paul, both of whom were murderers. He restored Joseph, the wrongly accused ex-con. He restored the mistress caught with the married man (John 8:1–11). He restored the kingdom of Israel time and time again after she disobeyed her Lord and followed after other gods. Jesus restored His eleven apostles, all of whom (except John) deserted Him during His greatest trial. And best of all, we too have been restored to God through the blood of Jesus.

Bookstores are full of self-help books that guide readers as to how to eliminate negative influences in their lives. This kind of instruction is what most counselors focus on and what most rehab programs teach. But true restoration takes root in our lives when our negatives are replaced by something. If we do not replace the negative with something positive, we will still have a hole in our lives, and that is why many people simply swap one bad habit for another. Removing the negative is not enough. Removing and then replacing is the answer.

Allow the power of the Lord to restore every damaged area of your life and to fill any void in you by His mighty Holy Spirit. Determine where any empty places are in your life and decide to fill them up with the things of the Lord. God will make flowers bloom in once-barren fields and cause streams to run in the desert (Isa. 43:19). "The end of a matter is better than its beginning" (Eccles. 7:8). Your end can become so much better than your beginning.

It is God's will to give us the desires of our heart.

David emphasized this: "May he give you the desire of your heart and make all your plans succeed" (Ps. 20:4), and again, "Delight yourself in the LORD and he will give you the desires of your heart" (Ps. 37:4). What well-loved verses these are. Everyone loves the idea of receiving the desires of their hearts, right? Then why is it that we do not all get what we want from God? The Lord never promised to answer a desire that was not conceived through the Holy Spirit. There are dreams and visions that the Lord has placed in us, and He will fulfill these dreams in us when we delight ourselves in Him. When God brings these desires to pass, they will bring life to us and will be a blessing. Welcome God's desires into your heart, and be willing to let go of anything that was born out of your own self-will.

Take a look at Psalm 20:4 again: "May he give you the desire of your heart and make all your plans succeed." Just a few lines down, in verse 7, God helps us to further understand this principle: "Some trust in chariots and some in horses, but we trust in the name of the LORD our God." King David was saying with this statement that he had put his trust in God alone—not in his army, his power, or his fighting men. We should do the same. Our desires should be supported by trust in God alone.

It is God's will to use us to further His kingdom.

"Jesus sent him away, saying, 'Return home and tell how much God has done for you.' So the man went away and told all over town how much Jesus had done for him" (Luke 8:38–39). After Jesus had healed the demon-possessed man in the region of the Gerasenes, Jesus told the man to go and tell others about the goodness of God. Telling others our story of redemption will further the kingdom of God and cause us to find the purpose behind our pain. The Lord has the ability to take any mess we are in and, once we are healed, to use our testimony for His glory.

Often the Lord will give us an assignment related to our area of healing. It seems as if everywhere I go I meet people who struggle with depression and anxiety. It's like I cannot go anywhere without God sending me these little heavenly assignments along my path. God allows people to open up to me so that I can minister to them. *Their need draws them to me through the Holy Spirit.*

When you meet others who need the kind of healing you have received, take it as an assignment from heaven. You are called to share out of the abundance you have within you. Part of your greater purpose is to use your struggles as well as your victories to draw others toward redemption and salvation in Christ.

"Praise the LORD, O my soul, and forget not all his benefits...who redeems your life from the pit and crowns you with love and compassion, who *satisfies your desires with good things* so that your youth is renewed like the eagle's" (Ps. 103:2, 4–5, emphasis added). So many believers remain unconvinced that God has good things in store for them. Mediocre things, maybe, but *good* things? There is tremendous fear among Christians that God keeps the good things for the special people or holds a lottery on blessings. The more good we do, the more raffle tickets we have in the bowl—and we only get the good stuff if our number comes up.

But all of us have equal access to the richness of God's blessings. How much we tap into the eternal is up to us, not up to a heavenly slot machine. Each of us can choose how close to Jesus we want to be, and He responds to any thirsty heart. Good things from the Father are available to you and to me as we seek after God with all our hearts. If you want to know God's will for your life, then become desperate. Desperate individuals always find God's plans and purposes for their lives.

Desperate people will find healing from depression. Desperate people knock on the windows of heaven until they open; desperate people call out to God in the middle of the night as the tears come. Desperate people keep going to Bible study even if they don't feel like going. Desperate people study the Bible until breakthrough comes. Desperate people go to God, because they know that He is the only answer.

FINDING SIGNIFICANCE

All of us go through seasons in which we wrestle with finding significance in life. All of humanity longs to find this secret ingredient whether in their personal, professional, or family lives. A focused life brings significance, but it is up to us to decide what we will focus on. If we focus on the world, our sense of significance will be wrapped up in the world. If we focus on God, our significance will be found in Him.

If you stay focused on depression, it is likely that depression will become your identity, and your level of significance will remain wrapped up in your ever-changing emotions. Proverbs 8:35 says, "For whoever finds me finds life." By focusing on knowing the Lord and His will for your life, you will uncover your true, God-given significance.

Dig Deeper

1. In what ways have you allowed others to make major decisions for you and not put enough weight on what the Lord is telling you to do?

2. List several "God desires" that the Lord has placed inside you.

3. When trials come, do you walk toward God, or do you tend to walk away from Him?

4. What does Scripture say that we should do in difficult times? How do you walk toward God during a great trial?

Assignments

Read Isaiah 55. Spend time praying that the Lord would give you a thirst for Him.

Exercise 1: Renew prayer in your life.

God does speak to us all day long, but we must have our spiritual ears tuned to His voice. Begin speaking to the Lord every day, all day long. Invite Him into your workplace, your commute, your laundry time. We do not have to wait until we are still in order to be alive in prayer. My husband says that he has a wonderful prayer time every time he works outside. There are many different types of prayers, and we are to operate in each of them as we have need.

Scripture tells us we are to be "praying always with all prayer and supplication in the Spirit" (Eph. 6:18, KJV). It also tells us that "the prayer of a righteous man is powerful and effective" (James 5:16). Renew your prayer life, and see the hand of God begin to change you and your circumstances! "I exhort therefore, first of all, that *supplications, prayers, intercessions, thanksgivings*, be made for all men; for kings and all that are in high place; that we may lead a tranquil and quiet life in all godliness and gravity" (1 Tim. 2:1–2, ASV, emphasis added).

Exercise 2: Relinquish control to God.

Make a list of things that you have tried to control but need to give to God. These may be really good things that you have held onto, believing that you were heading in the right direction. We control things anytime we fight to remain in the place of power over a situation or circumstance. But when we insist on maintaining control and put our position of control above the Lord's authority in our lives, we disobey God. What have you tried to be in control of? In order to reach the Lord's perfect will for your life, you must give God first place.

Prayer time

Spend time asking the Lord to put you into His perfect will for your life.

> *Lord, help me to hear Your voice clearly. Please give me direction and show me the path that You laid out for me before I was born. Fill me with Your desires for my life. I ask that You put people across my path to help me on my journey. Keep me on Your path through the promptings of the Holy Spirit. When trials come, help me to remain obedient to Your Word, and teach me how to turn to You when I am in need. Teach me how to pray. Show me how to hear Your voice. Make me a person of prayer. Show me what is around me or within me that can be used for me to walk out Your will for my life. Use me in many ways to bless others. In Jesus's name, amen.*

Chapter 10

SPEAK LIFE

May the words of my mouth and the meditation
of my heart be pleasing in your sight, O
LORD, my Rock and my Redeemer.
—*Psalm 19:14*

M Y HUSBAND AND I love cruises. I know, most cruise junkies have gray hair, but I am a sucker for the midnight dessert extravaganzas, the silly cruise games, and the towel animals the staff leaves on your bed. I even bought a cruise line's book on how to make those towel animals, so if you ever come stay with me, I will make you a towel monkey (that one's my favorite). One of Kevin's and my favorite cruises was the one we took to Alaska. We were by far the youngest people on this cruise (not counting the grandkids who came along with their grandparents) by about thirty years. We loved it. We even became friends with a sweet old couple whom we met in the mornings for early coffee. Different from the Caribbean cruises, on these Alaskan tours the ships hover close to the shoreline, which we enjoyed because we could get a glimpse of the wildlife down below.

One of the channels we sailed through took us to an amazing glacier that had a magnitude so magnificent that seeing it became an absolutely unforgettable moment for us. The waterway to the glacier was so tight that at times we felt as if we might be able to reach out and touch the sides of the cliff on either side of the ship. It was almost scary at certain moments—sometimes the ship was only yards away from the cliffs beside us. But we slipped perfectly through the corridor, on toward the glacier, and back out again. It's a pretty amazing stunt for this gigantic cruise ship to so gently and perfectly wind its way through those icy waters with such ease. And to think that all boats, large and small, are set on course by a relatively small device—a rudder. The Book of James in the New Testament says that our tongues are like little rudders. Just as a large ship can be steered by a very small rudder, so our tongues set the course for our lives.

I once heard that our relationship with the Lord is somewhat like a checker game. We take a turn, then the Lord has a turn; we take another turn, then He takes the next one. James describes it this way: "Come near to God and he will come near to you" (James 4:8). We are going to talk about something we can do when it's our turn—how we can make a move toward God.

The wonderful part about this move is that it is something we can do *today*. It doesn't require hours of prayer or help from friends—it is a decision we can make that the Word of God says will change our lives forever. But we have a choice to make: "This day I call heaven and earth as witnesses against you that *I have set before you life and death, blessings and curses. Now choose life*" (Deut. 30:19, emphasis added).

CHOOSE YOUR WORDS CAREFULLY

God wants us to know that the things we say really matter. By carefully examining the words that come out of our mouths, we can choose life and not death. This is not New Age, positive thinking, or even a doctrine of "name it, claim it" Christianity. This concept is an integral part of Scripture, taught to us from the beginning of God's relationship with humanity up until now. Speaking words of truth is a fundamental part of how the kingdom of God within us works and governs our lives.

Everything we say produces for us a crop. This fact is an eternal governing decree that we either walk in or walk away from. We either move with the current in the river of life, or we fight the movement of the stream and never progress downriver. It is that way with many of God's teachings, but especially so with this one. Our words are so powerful that they can greatly help or greatly hinder the direction of our lives. Many of you may be suffering from the fruit of your own negative words. Depression often produces negative words, which are the overflow of a depressed heart. Negative words will rot our souls over time. But when we change the way we speak, we will find that our healthy words will have influence over our countenance—and over the entire course of our lives.

It is so easy for us to use death-minded speech. Considering the negative influences all around us, it is no wonder that Christians often speak so much like the world. Unless we spend time hiding ourselves in the presence of the Lord, we will operate according to the world's systems without pausing to consider our ways. The world operates in a spirit of fear, negativity, and criticism. Most schools and workplaces are filled with language that is not uplifting to the people who hear it and not pleasing to God. But the Scripture tells us, "Put away perversity from your mouth; keep corrupt talk far from your lips" (Prov. 4:24). Surrounded as we are by a world full of poisonous messages, we need a complete detox from its corruption.

You may be thinking, "Of course I am negative! My life is a mess. How can I say anything good when everything seems so awful?" Keep reading, and I hope you won't feel the same way in a few minutes. Speaking life is not just about avoiding profane language or trying not to be negative. God's principles always apply to much more than behavior change. When we speak things forth, whether good or bad, we are putting our words into motion.

"He wore cursing as his garment; it entered into his body like water, into his bones like oil" (Ps. 109:18). Let us be wise and not wear cursing as a garment. This verse teaches us that when we speak forth words full of death, we pay a price. Death-filled words do ultimately enter into our souls like water, and they kill the work of the Spirit of God in us. On the other hand, words of life have great power and blessing attached to them.

"A wise man's heart guides his mouth" (Prov. 16:23). What guides your mouth? Do your words bring encouragement, respect, love, honor, faith, and blessing to you and to others? Or do your words bring criticism, rejection, fear, worry, and strife—and ultimately dig you deeper into the pit of anxiety and depression? "Pleasant words are a honeycomb, sweet to the soul and healing to the bones" (Prov. 16:24). Kind words are very sweet to the soul and can surely bring healing. Let your words be a blessing to others.

James 1:21 talks about "the word planted in you," referring to God's Word. But people too have the ability to plant words. Parents, every day you plant words inside your kids. What you plant in your children today will grow within them tomorrow. Wives, you plant into your spouse with each word you say. Your harvest will reflect your words. All of us, knowingly or unknowingly, plant into our family members, coworkers, friends, and others every day.

Proverbs 10:11 says, "The mouth of the righteous is a fountain of life." Our words can be a fountain of life-giving water to those around us, or they can accomplish a lifetime of damage.

TAMING THE TONGUE

Jesus had much to say about how we govern the words of our mouths. Read this next passage from Matthew very carefully, because in it Jesus reveals several very important principles:

> For out of the overflow of the heart the mouth speaks. The good man brings good things out of the good stored up in him, and the evil man brings evil things out of the evil stored up in him. But I tell you that men will have to *give account on the day of judgment for every careless word they have spoken*. For by your words you will be acquitted, and by your words you will be condemned.
> —MATTHEW 12:34–37, EMPHASIS ADDED

This statement is pretty radical. When I read it, I realize how I need to repent and make my words sweeter to the ears of God.

Jesus teaches us that the mouth speaks from the overflow of the heart. Without a pure heart, our words will not be pure. Even nice words, if they are spoken out of wrong motives, are displeasing to God. Remember that God always looks at the state of our hearts. Our words are a mirror to others of what is really inside us.

Jesus goes on in this passage to say that we will give an account for every careless word we have ever spoken. He said *every* careless word. Other translations refer to this as an "idle word." Either way, God is telling us that we cannot plead, "Oh, I was just having a bad day," or, "I didn't really mean to say that," when we stand before Him at the end of this life. There is not an excuse we can come up with that will make our "careless" words pleasing to Him. We can, however, decide to begin speaking words full of life and blessing—starting today. And like the rudder of a cruise ship, our tongues can begin to set us on a course of blessing and healing.

A good part of the Book of James is devoted to the "taming of the tongue." Let's look at what James has to teach us on this subject: "If anyone considers himself religious and yet does not keep a *tight rein on his tongue*, he deceives himself and *his religion is worthless*" (James 1:26, emphasis added). Wow, stinging words from the brother of Jesus. Being a disciple of Christ is about listening to God's instruction and then *putting into practice* what He asks us to do. James is letting us know that speaking words of life is extremely important in the kingdom of God, because when used selfishly, the tongue "corrupts the whole person" and "sets the whole course of his life on fire" (James 3:6).

James gives us another example, this one comparing our words to fresh water and salt water: "Can both fresh water and salt water flow from the same spring? My brothers, can a fig tree bear olives, or a grapevine bear figs? Neither can a salt spring produce fresh water" (James 3:11–12).

Adding salt to fresh water makes no sense—it would ruin the fresh water and make it unfit to drink. Even a small amount of salt corrupts a whole spring. We need to let the pure water of life fill us and cleanse us. Bathe in the purity of the Lord's waters, and be cleansed from all unrighteousness. Let your mouth and heart praise the Lord.

James, in the course of his instruction on this topic, compares the tongue to several visuals:

- The bit in a horse's mouth, which can turn the whole animal (James 3:3)

- A rudder, which can steer a large ship (James 3:4)

- A spark, which can set a forest afire (James 3:5)

When my husband and I visited Yosemite National Park one summer, the amazing scenery we saw in every direction captivated us. Luscious trees, rigid mountains, and cool streams made the landscape unforgettable. As we left the park to drive home and headed up through the mountain pass outside Yosemite, we saw that a huge area of the surrounding forest had been burned. For thousands of acres the landscape was full of half-burned black trees and dotted with shrubbery.

At our first stop we asked a ranger about the fire zone. We found out that a teenager had been target shooting in the area and had fired a gun in this very dry climate. His bullet had ricochet off a tree and sparked a flame. The boy had gotten nervous once the fire started, and he left the scene. What started as a tiny spark completely devastated the once-beautiful landscape, burning 34,000 acres and thirty homes. This is the picture that James wants us to associate with the tongue. Though small, our tongues can create great damage in our lives and in the lives of others.

Words Are Powerful

There are many ways in which we can speak words of life. Psalm 142:2–3 tells us one way: "I pour out my complaint before him; *before him I tell my trouble.* When my spirit grows faint within me, it is you who know my way" (emphasis added). In other words, *we need to talk with God, not people, about our problems.* Where do you pour out your complaints? Do you find yourself running to your friends the minute someone has bothered you? Do you talk behind your friends' backs when they have hurt you? Do you post nasty remarks on your Facebook page when your boss has made you crazy? We do need to vent when we are hurt or angry, but the Bible says that we are to take our complaints before the Lord. How differently would we handle situations if we always went to God *first*? I know doing so would have saved me from saying certain things that I later regretted.

Another way we can speak life is to be men and women of our word. James has something to say about this: "Let your 'Yes' be yes, and your 'No,' no" (James 5:12). In today's fast-paced society, it seems as if it is no big deal for people to back out on their word, to change their minds when they feel inconvenienced, or to say one thing but do another. This attitude has really come about since our grandparents' generation. In the first half of the twentieth century men and women generally tried their very best to keep their word, because they placed such value on good character. Now we have somehow gotten really lazy about keeping our word. If something better comes along, we are ready to ditch our obligations. Keep your word, and you will honor God and be an example of excellence to others.

Jesus knew how powerful words are. He saw His Father God create heaven and earth with the power of His words (Gen. 1). Jesus Himself is the Word of God made flesh (John 1:1–14). Jesus and His disciples did mighty miracles using the words that they spoke: "Get up!" "Be clean!" "Come out!" With just a few words, enough power was released in the name of Jesus to cast out demons, heal the sick, and make the blind see. Jesus gave His disciples (and us) the authority to do great things in the name of Jesus. We exercise that authority through the words that we speak in faith.

That is why so often the words that we say actually come to pass. Our words do hold authority. If you constantly talk about being sick, I bet you will be sick in no time. If you constantly say that you will never get married, then be careful, because you are speaking something forth, whether you realize it or not.

"Set a guard over my mouth, O LORD; keep watch over the door of my lips" (Ps. 141:3). We must watch our words carefully. Often people who struggle with depression are very negative in the way they speak. It is draining to be around negative people! I have several friends who are so negative that I find it difficult to be in their company. I love them, but I feel completely drained after I talk with them. I know that if I call them when I am having a bad day, I will get off the phone feeling worse than when I dialed their numbers. If we want to have—and keep—friends, we have to let go of negative words and complaining attitudes. It is completely overwhelming to the people around us when we have a constantly negative outlook. Make a decision to speak life and not death to those around you, and you will not only bless your own life but will also draw others to you.

WHAT DOES YOUR HEART SAY ABOUT YOU?

"For as he thinks in his heart, so is he" (Prov. 23:7, NKJV). We've been talking about the words we speak, but what about the words in our hearts, where no one else can hear what we say? For many people, this is the area of their lives that needs the greatest amount of healing. In the heart is the voice no one hears but you and God. What we verbalize in our hearts is what we *really* feel. The running tape that plays in the back of our minds and in the depths of our hearts tells the truth about what we are experiencing internally. Whatever we truly believe in our hearts about ourselves dictates everything else in our lives. God has actually programmed us to run that way. That is the main reason the Lord is so concerned with our hearts. Beyond wanting our obedience, the Lord knows that our heart-talk creates for us on the outside whatever is happening on the inside. What is your heart-talk saying?

Many people's hearts say degrading and destructive things. Sometimes we do this simply because of our own disappointment with ourselves. But in many cases people do it because of what someone else has done to them; they have come under the power of a controlling person and begun to think negatively about themselves.

But it is very important that we understand one thing: *no one can take our power from us; we* surrender *it.* This cannot be any more apparent than it is with women who stay in troubling relationships of any kind. In such situations there came a time at which an exchange of power took place. One person gave away power, and the other gladly took hold of it. If this describes you, *stop feeling powerless.* Please know that it is never too late to take your power back from the perpetrator of your pain.

Our minds and our spirits must be ready to believe words of truth and to walk in the path the Lord leads us in. *If we are caught up in a relationship that is unhealthy, we will often disregard the Lord's call in order to please the other person.* Giving up our power, giving up our opinions, and giving up our control to a person rather than to God always strips our souls as well as the power of God within us, and it leads us to speak false things about ourselves. This contributes to what is called a victim mentality, and it is very dangerous.

We will never be able to speak forth goodness if there are unwise thought patterns going on inside us. The way we think in our hearts will determine what we say and who we become (Prov. 23:7). It will be impossible for us to speak forth blessings over our lives if we are held captive to a victim mentality.

The victim mentality is one of the most common unhealthy behavioral patterns that depressed people struggle with. A victim mentality causes people to see everything through the context of something that hurt them long ago. They were once victims of some wrong, and over time the thought of what happened to them has crept into what they now believe about life.

The victim mentality may start out with a "poor me" attitude, but it can quickly turn into something that causes much more damage within a person's heart. When we take on this kind of thought process and the negative speaking it produces, we are completely stopped from moving forward and taking responsibility for our own actions. Satan wants us to maintain our victim mentality so that we are not able to function normally within the kingdom of God and can never escape the web of depression.

Do you have a victim mentality? Read the statements below; if you find yourself saying or believing a few of them, then you are living with a victim mentality in some area of your life:

- Why does nothing good happen to me?

- Why does everyone take advantage of me?

- The things that have happened in my life are not my fault.

- God never seems to answer my prayers.

- I often expect the worst.

- I find myself looking to others to give me what only God can give.

- I am a needy person.

People with a victim mentality always have a fire raging in some area of their lives. And they believe that someone else has caused these major disasters—that the problems are never caused by their own actions.

There are several very negative results of this thought process. First, a victim mentality steals people's ability to believe that God is good. Next, it causes people to believe that nothing will change or ever get better in their lives. They give up on trying to change because they believe that no matter what they do, the results will ultimately be bad. Again, this is partly due to not taking responsibility for the direction in which their lives are going, and ultimately, this manner of thinking and speaking turns into a habit and becomes part of who these people are and how they view life. The victim's negative responses to hardships are often very pronounced or highly exaggerated. And finally, people with a victim mentality are attracted to perpetrators who will further encourage their behavior.

I have counseled with many women who are controlled by a victim mentality. One young woman I began to help was unstable financially and suffered from emotional issues. After ministering to her for a period of weeks, I began to see that her problems had nothing to do with her needs. Her problem was a victim mentality, and I knew that as long as she maintained that mind-set, she would always be in the middle of a disaster. Nothing was ever this woman's fault, and she was not to blame for her current situation or her poor decisions. She began to put unreasonable expectations on our relationship, asking me to buy her things, asking me to find her a better job, asking me to buy her gas, and wanting all my time and attention. This young woman focused only on the things I had not given her, not on the many things that I had done for her. When I did not fulfill her expectations, she actually called the church to complain about me not ministering to her needs!

In this woman's mind I owed her, because she was a victim of life and I was not. Nothing that the church or I did for her was ever enough. Now this is a case of an extreme victim mentality that was completely out of control, but I see women all the time who struggle with a victim mentality to much lesser degrees.

I hope today that if you do suffer from this mentality, you see that you have a choice about your future. You are standing at a fork in the road. You can continue walking through life as a victim, or you can become an overcomer. But you cannot be both. You must decide your next steps.

God desires to bring continual increase and prosperity to our souls and our lives. A victim mentality staggers our ability to receive from God, so if you are living with this mind-set, you could unknowingly be cutting off the valve to your heavenly source. The truth is, all of us can find reasons to be a victim, as the twists and turns of life don't always seem fair. Depression will always want you to be a slave to a victim mentality. It tells you, "You could have such a great life if it wasn't for..." This is a lie, and we must begin to see that this is not God's plan for His people. He has made us to be overcomers in this life, not needy people looking to others to change our lot in life. "You, dear children, are from God and have *overcome* them, *because the one who is in you is greater than the one who is in the world*" (1 John 4:4, emphasis added).

People With a Victim Mentality	Overcomers
Say, "It's never my fault."	Say, "What can I change about my actions?"
Think, "The things done to me set the course for my life."	Think, "The Holy Spirit alone sets the course of my life."
Blame others and are slow to repent	Take responsibility for actions and are quick to repent
Believe that bad things have lasting effects	Believe that bad things are momentary and that God will soon bless them
Have lost hope	Are full of hope
Look to others to light a fire within them	Look for ways to light fires within others
Are self-centered	Are focused on others first
Always have a problem	Are problem-solvers
Look to others to give them justice and think people owe them	Look to God for their justice
Offer excuses	Display a spirit of honesty
Allow others to crush their vision	Maintain vision for their own lives
Believe that everywhere they go, something bad will happen	Believe that everywhere they go, they walk in favor
Give up	Bounce back
Are ungrateful	Have a thankful heart

A victim mentality separates us from the blessings available to us in the kingdom of God. But operating as an overcomer will activate blessings for us. Choose to have an attitude that embraces the best that God has to give you. Confess faith and speak life.

Dig Deeper

- Do you talk about your problems on a daily basis (for months at a time)?

- Do your conversations focus primarily on you?

- When you spend time with other people, do you look to them to make you feel better?

- Have people told you that you are a negative person? (If you are unsure, ask three people to give you their opinions.)

- Are you critical about almost everything?

- Do you think that your negativity has affected your relationships?

- If you answered yes to many of these questions, you have a habit of speaking words that are not life giving. How will you change?

  1. How will you begin to change your speech to make it more life giving?

  2. Why are the words we speak so important?

  3. What do you control by the words you speak?

  4. What guides your mouth most of the time?

  5. What does it mean to set a guard over your mouth (Ps. 141:3)?

Assignments

Read the Book of James. List three reasons it is important to the Lord that we use life-giving words.

Exercise 1: Speak life.

"A wise man's heart guides his mouth, and his lips promote instruction" (Prov. 16:23). Do you speak life-giving words or words full of death? Go on a fast from speaking any words that do not profess faith. Focus on maintaining a positive perspective, and let your words mirror your new attitude.

Exercise 2: Let go of any victim mentality you have.

"I have told you these things, so that in me you may have peace. In this world you will have trouble. But take heart! *I have overcome the world*" (John 16:33, emphasis added). If you identified yourself as someone who is operating in a victim mentality, release this thought process from your life.

Prayer time

> *Lord, I come to You now, asking You to release me from operating in any form of victim mentality. I am not a victim. I believe that You have given me the spirit of an overcomer, and I desire to operate with a new mind-set and heart. Help me to take responsibility for myself and to walk in accountability. I pray that Your Holy Spirit will teach me how to operate with a mind that is set on You and is not focused on my problems. I can do all things through You, Lord. In Jesus's name, amen.*

Chapter 11

RESIST THE DEVIL

Resist the devil, and he will flee from you.
—James 4:7

WHEN I WAS growing up, my family always had plenty of pets around, especially stray cats that had made our backyard their permanent home. On a particular occasion one of these adopted cats had hurt her paw, and since she was untrained and therefore unable to come in the house, my parents let her heal in the little shed behind our home. This would keep her from running around on her paw, and we could keep a better eye on her while she healed. But after a few days of this my parents became alarmed, because even though they were bringing the cat food, her bowl had gone untouched. After some observation, however, they discovered that the cat was not the only one locked inside that shed.

Unknowingly my dad had locked a raccoon in there too! That poor cat had stayed way up in the rafters for days, never coming down to eat, because she was petrified with fear. Whenever my dad came in to see about the cat those first few days, the raccoon would hide. Of course, we laughed and felt so sorry for that poor cat that had been locked up for days with the raccoon.

Fear keeps us paralyzed, as it did that poor cat up on the rafters. The devil works to assail us through people and through circumstances, and both lines of attack can create a mountain of fear within us. Depression is partly rooted in fear, and when you find yourself up on a rafter with a raccoon below staring you down, it feels awfully hard to resist the devil. So how do we resist the devil during those times when we feel so overwhelmed? It is in these times especially that we must learn to stand against him.

LEARNING HOW TO FIGHT

What does it mean to resist the devil? I am sure that many believers have heard "Resist the devil, and he will flee from you" numerous times, yet when I look around, I do not see a whole lot of resisting taking place within the church.

We must embrace the fact that there is a real devil that needs resisting. He hates us. He wants us to be miserable, angry, and selfish. He plants destruction in the minds of men and women, and he causes chaos on the earth. When we are under attack, it is not a person who desires to do evil toward us — it is the devil at work within the life of the person attacking. We need to stop being angry with people, place blame rightly on the devil, and fight against him.

> For our struggle is not against flesh and blood, but against the rulers, against the authorities, against the powers of this dark world and against the spiritual forces of evil in the heavenly realms.
> —EPHESIANS 6:12

This verse scares a lot of people. Fear is a big reason that a majority of the church runs away when the words *spiritual warfare* are mentioned. It may seem scary to us to think of a spiritual realm in which demons and angels battle all around us, and since we cannot see this realm with our eyes, it can be easy to dismiss. Don't let your fears keep you in ignorance about this very important subject in Scripture. Jesus and His disciples had to confront the devil and his demons head-on, and we must do it as well. Depression and anxiety are not from God, but they come from the hand of the devil, our adversary. If we don't know the cause of the battles in our lives, we will spend time fighting against people rather than against our true enemy. *Our real fight is against these demonic strongholds.*

> For though we live in the world, we do not wage war as the world does. *The weapons we fight with are not the weapons of the world.* On the contrary, they have divine power to demolish *strongholds*
> —2 CORINTHIANS 10:3–4, EMPHASIS ADDED

Our war is not with our rebellious child, our mean sister-in-law, our ex-husband, or our grumpy neighbor. No, the Bible tells us that all our struggles, both within ourselves and with others, are from the hand of the evil one. It is the devil that tempts people with evil thoughts and is at the root of the attacks on the children of God.

Most Christians probably believe this on some level but are not sure what to do about it. The idea of warfare can be intimidating, even to a Christian who has been in the faith for many years. Whether you have been saved for a few weeks or for many years, *now* is the time for you to take up the sword of the Lord and to battle for what is rightfully yours. Jesus died to bring peace to our souls and to abolish anxiety forever. It is time for you to battle against the darkness so that you can receive the inheritance set aside for you.

We do not need to fear the words of warfare that we read in Ephesians, because we have been given great power through the Lord Jesus. He has anointed us with power from on high

(Luke 24:49) and given us "authority to trample on snakes and scorpions [any demonic power] and to overcome all the power of the enemy" (Luke 10:19). Amen! God has not left us without weapons nor without the power to wield those weapons.

The night before Jesus was crucified, He had many things to tell His disciples about what was going to take place after He left to be with His Father. Jesus knew His time was short. At this point in the Gospel of John, Judas the betrayer had already left the Passover dinner to gather together the mob that would arrest Jesus. Jesus then spent some very personal time with the remaining eleven disciples and gave His final words to His friends. He told them that they would be kicked out of their synagogues (John 16:2) and would become hated and persecuted for His sake (John 15:18–25)—heavy words from their rabbi.

Jesus wanted the disciples to have hope and faith, even in the face of the coming trials. Just hours before He was arrested, He shared with them about the mighty gift He was going to send them, the Spirit of truth (John 14:17). He also comforted the disciples, saying, "I have told you these things, so that in me you may have peace. In this world you will have trouble. *But take heart! I have overcome the world*" (John 16:33, emphasis added).

These words are also for us as we face trials and attacks of many kinds. No matter what we face, Jesus has overcome the enemy. And since we are seated with Christ in heavenly places (Eph. 2:6), we have overcome with Him! Do not fear your enemy, but know instead that he has already been defeated. Depression, anxiety, fear, and insecurity are no match for Christ. Attacks are bound to come our way, so let us be alert, wise, and anointed to fight against the powers of darkness.

Since we are in a spiritual fight, we must choose to fight

with spiritual weapons. Let's look specifically into how we can resist the devil so that he will flee.

OBEDIENCE

Disobedience opens the door to the demonic in our life. This is a *huge* concept to apply to our lives. God fights for His kids when His kids are obedient. Time and time again Israel fought against terrifying armies as Moses led the people toward the Promised Land. When the Israelites were obedient to the Lord, God did amazing works to defeat the idol-worshipping kingdoms. God even made the sun stand still for an entire day during the battle of Gilgal when Joshua had to fight against five Amorite kings and their armies (Josh. 10:1–15). When Israel was disobedient, however, they often met defeat. I don't know about you, but I would sure welcome some sun-stand-still miracles in my life. God comes out to fight our battles when we serve Him through obedience.

Believers, though saved through Jesus, can still piddle around in darkness by walking in sin and depending on what the world has to offer. But listen to what James had to say about that: "You adulterous people, don't you know that friendship with the world is hatred toward God?" (James 4:4).

Let's take another look at the verse quoted at the beginning of this chapter, this time with its preceding statement: "*Submit yourselves, then, to God.* Resist the devil, and he will flee from you" (James 4:7, emphasis added). This reads differently now, doesn't it? As we go forward, remember that it is pointless for us to do a bunch of "resisting" if we remain unsubmitted to the Lord. *Submitting to the Lord gives us the power to resist the devil.* We need to be careful that we are not resisting in our own power. Doing so will cause us to become really weary and give up. If you have recently given up in resisting the devil, if you have come to believe that it is pointless to fight him, then check your life to be sure that you have been faithful to the Lord in obedience and submission. Fix any problems you discover, and your spiritual battles will become easier for you to fight.

Waiting on the Lord

Most of the time when we enter into a battle, there is a period of waiting until we reach the battle's conclusion. You might be thinking, "How in the world will waiting help anything?" But throughout Scripture the Lord tells us again and again to wait upon Him. To us, waiting is simply passing the time until we get something that we want, but biblical waiting is altogether different.

Biblical waiting is full of activity; it is not wasted time. Even Jesus had to wait in obedience to His Father. I wonder how long Jesus knew that He was the Messiah before He launched His ministry at age thirty-three? Perhaps He could have commanded miracles when He was six or cast out demons when he was two, but He didn't. Jesus's father Joseph passed away sometime between the time Jesus was twelve and when He began his ministry at age thirty. As Jesus watched His earthly dad pass away, as much as He may have wanted to, He stood back and did not use His God-power to raise Joseph from the dead. It was not yet Jesus's time. Jesus had to wait to reveal His true identity until the Father's perfect time, even though it meant losing a member of His family. But waiting is not without purpose. It is an important factor in God's kingdom, and God stresses that to us again and again:

Wait for the LORD; be strong and take heart and wait for
the LORD.
—PSALM 27:14

Be still before the LORD and wait patiently for him.
—PSALM 37:7

Be still, and know that I am God.
—PSALM 46:10

Waiting on the Lord means choosing not to make something happen for ourselves outside God's will for us. Abraham
wanted a child so badly that he slept with his maidservant,
even though God had told him that his wife Sarah would bear
him a child. Abraham just couldn't stand the wait.

Many times in my life I have nearly missed God because
I became impatient for Him to work. I have bought so many
things that I didn't actually like because I couldn't find what I
really wanted or couldn't afford the better item. I would have
ended up happier with my purchases if I had waited for the
right things to come along. Impatience will cause us to make
wrong decisions. Impatience is also a form of selfishness. It
says to God, "Hey, I don't like Your timing. I think I can
figure this out better myself!"

Often the Lord will give us a promise far in advance of its
fulfillment. God's Word says that each of His promises has an
appointed time to be fulfilled and that if we wait, it will come
to pass: "For the revelation awaits an *appointed time*; it speaks
of the end and will not prove false. *Though it linger, wait for it*;
it will certainly come and will not delay" (Hab. 2:3, emphasis
added). God's timing is often not even close to our desired
timing, thus the frustration on our part. But we have to be
willing to surrender our timeline and to find contentment

during the wait, no matter how long it takes. This will frustrate the plans that the devil has for us.

Our willingness to wait on the Lord will abort any plans and distractions the devil has planned for our lives. Satan loves to dangle a false carrot in front of us right at the time we are about to give up. It is easy for us to take the carrot from the devil, even if we know in our hearts that we shouldn't. For example, many Christians are in dating relationships. They really want to do the right thing and wait until marriage to have sex, and they begin well, but then the wait gets to feel really long. Then here comes Satan dangling that carrot.

We would avoid so many messes if we would be obedient in the wait. A believer willing to wait on the Lord is *not* an easy target for the devil. The enemy may try to strike a few blows to such a Christian, but after a while he will realize that this believer will not be moved from faith, and he will eventually give up. Many Christians do not conquer simply because they tire out and therefore forfeit God's best.

Some of the most difficult times we will ever face as believers will be times of great waiting on the Lord. Satan can more easily disarm us when we are waiting *without exercising faith*. That's why when we are in a great battle and our faith is being challenged, it seems that the blows from the devil increase. The wait in the battle has made us weary, so the enemy strikes again, creating a bigger battle.

Wait with a valiant heart. Do not lower your stance just because the wait seems longer than you first thought it would be. Fill your waiting with faith. Take a stand and decide that you will not grow impatient with God's plans. Do not let the devil convince you to take a bite of his carrot. Anything that God has promised us is worth the wait.

RESISTING TEMPTATION

A few months ago the only verse I could have recited about temptation would have been the one from the Lord's Prayer that says, "And lead us not into temptation, but deliver us from the evil one" (Matt. 6:13). The last phrase of the Lord's Prayer is so familiar to us that we can almost recite it without thinking through the words of the prayer. That's what happens when we read the Word of God with only our minds. The Word does not come alive to us without the Spirit of God breathing through it.

I will admit that I had not prayed very much about temptation until recently, when the Lord gave me deeper revelation in this area. The Lord's Prayer, given by Jesus to His disciples, is an outline for us on how to pray to the Father God in a meaningful way. Tucked into the end of this prayer is quite a big revelation about the meaning and importance of temptation. When I paired this teaching with other scriptures on the same topic, the picture Jesus was presenting became very clear to me, and I realized that I had been missing out on a powerful prayer. Let's see what Jesus wanted us to grasp.

When we say "lead us not into temptation," as the Lord's Prayer states, we must first realize that the Lord is not the One who presents evil temptations to us. "When tempted, no one should say, 'God is tempting me.' For God cannot be tempted by evil, nor does he tempt anyone" (James 1:13). Any evil thing cannot come from the Lord and therefore comes from Satan, the father of lies. Instead, the phrase "lead us not into temptation" is more like saying, "God, do not permit me to fall into or experience temptation." When read that way, we see that God has the ability, when we pray, to actually keep us from experiencing a temptation that could be harmful to us.

When we are struggling with depression, it is very easy for us to fall prey to harmful temptations. We talked in chapter 2 about false comforts. These are temptations that promise to make us feel better but will eventually cause destruction in our lives. Other temptations consist of self-harm, self-hate, and suicide. Praying for God's protection and deliverance from these temptations should be a daily part of our prayer lives.

Pray for God's invisible hand to put up a barrier of protection around you that will deter temptations of the devil from coming into your life. All of us need the Lord to protect us from temptation that we could walk into, either knowingly or unknowingly. We need this protection because temptation is the starting line for all sin. Every sin starts out rather small, sometimes so small that we don't even bother to deal with it. If we do not choose to do something about these seemingly small thoughts that developed from a temptation the devil presented to us, it can later cause major trauma in our souls.

This verse gives us a process for all sin patterns: "Each one is tempted when, by his own evil desire, he is dragged away and enticed. Then, after desire has conceived, it gives birth to sin; and sin, when it is full-grown, gives birth to death" (James 1:14–15). Let's dissect these six steps.

STEP	What happens in a person's spirit	What happens in a person's life outwardly
1	We are tempted.	We are *exposed* to a particular sin.
2	We are dragged away and enticed.	We allow the sin to *grab our attention,* and we allow it *into our thoughts and our minds.*
3	Our desire has conceived.	We think about actually doing the sin.
4	Our desire gives birth to sin.	We *act out* or *partake of* the sin.

STEP	What happens in a person's spirit	What happens in a person's life outwardly
5	Our sin becomes full-grown.	We *repeat the sin* over and over until it matures in our lives.
6	Our sin gives birth to death.	We become spiritually dead because of our disobedience.

We are exposed to sin every day, all day long. It is intro-
duced to us through television, the Internet, within conversation, and, most importantly, within our own minds. These
six steps can be taken within a matter of seconds, or they can
build for years. The first step, as we have seen, is that Satan
introduces a thought into our minds. This is the point at
which we need to act. Just because a thought comes to our
minds doesn't mean we have to allow it in. We have the power
to simply refuse it when it is first presented to us. If we do not,
we take the second step and allow the sinful thought to hold
our attention.

"We demolish arguments and every pretension that sets itself
up against the knowledge of God, and *we take captive every
thought to make it obedient to Christ*" (2 Cor. 10:5, emphasis
added). If you struggle with your thought life, memorize this
verse. This truth is spiritual bread for us to feast on. I have
heard people say, "I just can't help what I think about." This
is simply not true. God would not ask us to take captive every
thought if we were not able to do it. Just because we have not
taken captive our thoughts before does not mean that we do
not have the ability to do it. We can do all things through
Christ (Phil. 4:13).

God does not ask us to take captive every demon or stronghold. No, we are only asked to "take captive every *thought*
to make it obedient to Christ." This is a matter of obedience.
Jesus gave us the power to do it. If we do not take captive that

evil thought (or temptation), we will move on to the third step and begin developing a plan of action to carry it out. We will see ourselves committing the act, and we will plan how we can make it happen. From this point on sin is taking place.

Not only is the act of sin itself displeasing to the Lord, but also our lingering on the thought dishonors Him. Jesus said in Matthew 5:27–28, "You have heard that it was said, 'Do not commit adultery.' But I tell you that anyone who looks at a woman lustfully has already committed adultery with her in his heart." Our thoughts matter very much and are often used as temptation bait by the devil.

The way to stop this cascade is for us to stay away from things that would draw us toward sin. If we are confronted by temptation, however, we must then take authority over any sinful thought. Ask God to keep you from temptation, as He suggested in His prayer outline, the Lord's Prayer. As an old Jewish saying puts it, "You cannot forbid a bird to fly over your head, but you can certainly forbid it to make a nest in your hair." When temptations come, make sure they do not make a nest within your heart.

Depression comes as a temptation to many people, and once we allow it into our minds and hearts, it begins to take root. For those of you struggling with depression, hundreds of negative, consuming thoughts try to become embedded in your conscious mind. It takes discipline and resolve for people struggling with depression to begin to do something about these thoughts that plague them every day. Once we recognize these unhealthy or self-destructive thoughts, we have to take action immediately.

Let's look once more at the end of 2 Corinthians 10:5: "We take captive every thought to make it obedient to Christ." This scripture tells us two things to do with a thought once it is identified as destructive. First, we must take it captive, and second, we are told to make it obedient to Christ. To take a thought captive means to arrest that thought and to expel it from our minds. This takes less than a second. As soon as the thought arrives, act quickly to escort it right back out of your mind. Then replace that thought with one that is in obedience to the Word of God.

For example, this thought is presented to your mind: "My life is never going to get better." Immediately cast it from your mind and then tell yourself the truth, based upon the Word of God. We need to do more than acknowledge that we are having a negative thought—we need to do something proactive about it. We must quickly replace that thought by saying, "No, that is not true. I have the mind of Christ. He is my healer, and He has a good life for me. Things will get better."

At first this may take you a minute or two to sort out in your mind, especially if you have never taken captive your thoughts before. But as you learn to walk in this powerful principle, you will become faster at turning the tide of depressed thoughts and will begin to walk in a greater measure of freedom.

Because depression is such a battle of the mind, I cannot underscore this life-giving tool enough. Just the other day I was talking with a woman from my church who has a wrecked thought life. She struggles with constant insecurity, and her mind is always on a negative treadmill, repeating the same harmful thoughts day after day. "I can't help what I think about," she told me. "My mind won't turn off. I don't know how to think on good things because I have been like this for so long. I don't know how to change."

Depression, fear, anxiety, and insecurity will keep us on a hamster wheel of self-loathing until we decide to do something different. We choose what we think on. Our thoughts are under our control. Try putting 2 Corinthians 10:5 into practice right now by taking captive any negative thought you have and replacing it with a thought that is obedient to Christ. If you choose to do this for thirty days, your life will change—guaranteed. Try God's Word out, and see for yourself if it works. Resist the devil by resisting temptation and by setting a watchtower over your thought life.

GUARDING YOUR HEART

"Above all else, guard your heart, for it is the wellspring of life" (Prov. 4:23, emphasis added). This may be one of the most important scriptures and concepts throughout our entire study. *Above all else.* That means to put this instruction at the top of the pile, to circle it and highlight it and contemplate its value.

This verse says that the heart is "the wellspring of life." What a beautiful description of how our hearts function in the spirit. A spring gives water, and water gives life. Without water, all living things die. Our hearts, in the same way, water the rest of our being. Our hearts provide for us the most essential elements for life. In the Scriptures water is a picture of life in the Spirit and the bounty of the Lord. It is of utmost importance that we guard our hearts, this valuable treasure, because it is the source of everything that flows into our lives.

James says that we must keep ourselves from "being polluted by the world" (James 1:27). In order to stay away from this pollution, we have to be aware of what we allow to be put in front of us. Jesus said, "The eye is the lamp of the body. If your eyes are good, your whole body will be full of light. But if your eyes are bad, your whole body will be full of darkness" (Matt. 6:22–23). We cannot expect to have pure hearts when our eyes and ears are filled with the world's trash. What are you watching, listening to, or reading that could contaminate you?

"Therefore, get rid of all moral filth and the evil that is so *prevalent*" (James 1:21, emphasis added). Well said, James. The fact that evil is prevalent and everyone around us is so casual about it does not mean that Christians have a pass to partake of it. Guarding our hearts is a full-time job. We cannot take a day off, and we can't sleep late. Our hearts are a hidden garden that needs watering with the Word of God and pruning of the weeds that can begin to sprout in it. Many women suffer from depression yet watch TV programs that make them feel worse, listen to music that feeds negative thoughts, and hang out with people who make them feel badly about themselves. When women stop feeding on the garbage that heightens their depression, healing comes more easily.

The devil can make his way into our lives through unholy media, filthy words, or disturbing thoughts. Do not be fooled into thinking that exposure to these things does not affect us. We open wide a door for Satan when we welcome garbage into our hearts. Remember that we are always feeding our souls something. If we are not feasting on the Word of God and receiving life from the Spirit, then we might be filling up on the things of the world.

Do as the psalmist did: "I will walk in my house with blameless heart…I will have nothing to do with evil" (Ps. 101:2, 4). Shut the door to your heart and allow only God to have the key. Erect a wall around your heart and stand guard against the enemy. Whenever your wall is breached, close it again through prayer, asking the Lord for forgiveness, and then stand guard once again. Resist the devil by allowing him no access into your heart.

The Power of Prayer

"And God raised us up with Christ and seated us with him in the heavenly realms in Christ Jesus" (Eph. 2:6). Spiritual warfare is simply using the power and authority that Jesus gave us through His death and resurrection. As I studied the Gospels recently, I took note of how often the Scriptures said, "But Jesus often withdrew to lonely places and prayed" (Luke 5:16). In just one of the Gospels it was referenced that Jesus went away to secret places to pray at least nine times. Jesus had a lifestyle of seeking quiet time with the Lord, despite a hectic schedule. He had to get away from the business of His ministry so He could sit alone with His Father. Jesus had the most important career of anyone who ever walked the earth, yet He created time to pray. Our lives cannot be so filled with daily clutter that we do not take a break in order to spend time in prayer before the Lord.

Prayer is a most valuable resource in fending off an attack of the devil. We have the ability to defeat evil because Jesus gave us authority over darkness and the power to do the kinds of things He had done (John 14:12). Jesus said, "I have given you *authority to...overcome all the power of the enemy*; nothing will harm you" (Luke 10:19, emphasis added). We exercise the power that Jesus gave us by speaking God's Word over the strongholds—by attacking the darkness. Learn how to attack the enemy through prayer. Break the power of the enemy in your life.

One problem we tend to struggle with, especially when we are depressed, is anxiety. But the Scriptures tell us, "Do not be *anxious* about anything, but in everything by *prayer* and supplication with thanksgiving let your requests be made known to God. And the peace of God, which surpasses all understanding, will *guard your hearts and your minds* in Christ Jesus" (Phil. 4:6–7, ESV, emphasis added). If we are anxious about something, this scripture tells us to bring it to the Lord in prayer. We need to ask the Lord *how* to pray about this area of our lives. We need to ask Him to *reveal to us what we are battling* in the spirit. When God speaks to us, we then go into prayer and battle the enemy using the power that Jesus gave us. We must seek out our authority.

There are a lot of books on this subject of spiritual warfare, and the more we understand how to do spiritual battle, the more effective we will be in combat. Let us model the behavior of Jesus. Let us take to our prayer closets (or cars or kitchens) and resist the devil through prayer. "Therefore I tell you, whatever you ask for in prayer, believe that you have received it, and it will be yours" (Mark 11:24).

Dig Deeper

1. What did Jesus mean when He said, "I have overcome the world" (John 16:33)?

2. What authority did Jesus give to believers?

3. Have you been scared of "spiritual warfare" in the past? If so, why?

4. What does it mean to conduct "spiritual warfare" in prayer?

5. What does it mean to "guard your heart"?

6. How do you need to guard your heart?

Assignments

Read Ephesians 6:10–20. Second Corinthians 10:4 tells us, "The weapons we fight with are not the weapons of the world." Which weapons does the Christian have against the enemy? Write down the armor that we wear through the Spirit of God.

Exercise 1: Identify your triggers.

As we have studied, guarding our hearts is of utmost importance if we want to remain full of joy and free from the trappings of the devil. Guarding your heart will become easier for you as you identify the specific triggers that most easily cause the walls of your heart to come down. For example, when I was breaking free from depression and anxiety, I realized that after I watched certain TV shows, I felt worse. I found that if I watched talk shows about depression or interviews with depressed people, I immediately felt different and was pulled down as well. I decided that I would always turn the channel when something like this came on the TV.

Think through your life and identify which activities, media, conversations, or people affect your outlook negatively. You know that something is a trigger for you if *every time* you are exposed to it, you feel the walls of your heart coming down and the weight of depression or anxiety increasing. Spend some time asking the Lord to show you the things that trigger depression or anxiety. Then write them down. After you have made your list, decide to adjust your life so as to limit your exposure to these depression triggers.

Exercise 2: Take captive your negative thoughts.

"We demolish arguments and every pretension that sets itself up against the knowledge of God, and *we take captive every thought to make it obedient to Christ*" (2 Cor. 10:5, emphasis added). God has given all of us the ability to decide what we will think about and meditate on. In the lives of those who are depressed, the battle that is most often fought is within the mind. The mind becomes the battleground where we can either win or lose the war. To win the war, you must start practicing and training your mind to take captive every thought that is not aligned with the will of the Lord. Rather than dwelling on these negative thoughts, decide to take them captive the moment they come to you, and cast them out of your mind. Redirect your thoughts toward something that will be a blessing to you.

> Finally, brothers, whatever is *true*, whatever is *noble*, whatever is *right*, whatever is *pure*, whatever is *lovely*, whatever is *admirable*—if anything is *excellent* or *praiseworthy*—think about such things. Whatever you have learned or received or heard from me, or seen in me—*put it into practice*. And the God of peace will be with you.
> —Philippians 4:8–9, emphasis added

The Lord gives us a list of healthy thoughts in the scripture above. If any of your thoughts cannot be described by the words in this list, make a decision to push them out of your mind and refuse to dwell on them. Dwelling on an unhealthy topic can be very destructive. It is like what happens to a snowball rolling down an embankment. The snowball may start out small, but eventually it gets bigger and bigger, until it is unstoppable. Philippians 4:9 says we need to put these things into practice. Your assignment is to practice taking captive your unhealthy thoughts. Identify them, and then take time to deal with them.

Prayer time

Spend time in prayer and practice resisting the devil.

Lord, I come before You and ask You to show me how to resist the enemy. Lord, please put a wall around my heart and help me to guard it. I pray that You will keep me from temptation and that You will keep my heart pure toward You. I ask that You show me how to keep my thought life obedient to Christ and how to keep my mind full of excellent thoughts. Teach me also how to identify unhealthy thought patterns and help me to cast them out of my mind. Help me to stand against the devil and to fight for the kingdom of God. In Jesus's name, amen.

Chapter 12

LOVE OTHERS

This is my command: Love each other.
—*John 15:17*

WHEN I LOOK back over my life thus far, I can see that my biggest wounds have been inflicted by friendly fire. When I was in high school, it was a sister in Christ who attacked me and made my senior year extremely difficult. When I was in college, it was a sister in Christ who betrayed me and broke my heart. I have forgiven these people, but my point is that so many of us in the church do not love others as we should. I don't always love as I should. Jesus told us that in the last days "the love of most will grow cold" (Matt. 24:12). For the church of Christ to be triumphant in these last days, we have to learn to love people now more than ever.

The Father's heart is that we may radically experience the love of God and then radically reveal that love to others. But there is a great war raging within our hearts. The enemy desires that we hold grudges, break fellowship, show favoritism, and harbor hate within our hearts. When we walk out our Christian life without love, we are crippled in the spirit.

Jesus taught us how to love: "Remain in me, and I will remain in you.... As the Father has loved me, so have I loved you. Now remain in my love" (John 15:4, 9). Our mission is to remain in the Father's love. When we operate outside His love, we have a very difficult time loving others or putting them first. To successfully put others before ourselves, we must be plugged into the Father. Jesus calls this remaining in Him. Remaining in Jesus means that we are conscious of His love and His presence and that we actively seek to share His life with others throughout our day.

Jesus often taught messages using the landscape around Him as an example. Using a picture that would have been very familiar to His disciples, Jesus taught His disciples what it meant to remain in Him. "No branch can bear fruit by itself; *it must remain in the vine*. Neither can you bear fruit unless you remain in me. *I am the vine; you are the branches*. If a man remains in me and I in him, he will bear much fruit; apart from me you can do nothing" (John 15:4–5, emphasis added). We receive all our spiritual nutrients by remaining a part of the Father's vine. Apart from the vine, loving others is impossible.

LOVE IS EVERYTHING

> If I speak in the tongues of men and of angels, but have not love, I am only a resounding gong or a clanging cymbal. If I have the gift of prophecy and can fathom all mysteries and all knowledge, and if I have a faith that can move mountains, but have not love, I am nothing. If I give all I possess to the poor and surrender my body to the flames, *but have not love, I gain nothing.*
> —1 CORINTHIANS 13:1–3, EMPHASIS ADDED

Without love all our spiritual gifts, ministry, and talents are worthless. That is why when we see people ministering without love, we can get so turned off by their approach. Serving people without love feels like work; there is no joy in it. The apostle Paul writes, "And now these three remain: faith, hope and love. *But the greatest of these is love*" (1 Cor.

13:13, emphasis added). Love is the hinge pin, love is the secret ingredient, and love is the true measure of a person.

When my grandmother was in the hospital for several weeks, she was helped by a dear woman whose job was to bathe the patients inside the ICU. This woman's job was certainly not a glamorous one and didn't bring in the biggest salary. But my mom watched her carefully bathe my grandmother, and as she bathed her, she spoke kind words to her and gently rubbed her legs to improve circulation. This woman took such tender care of my grandmother, whom she did not even know, that my mom told her what a wonderful job she was doing. This woman replied, "I lost both my parents early in life. When I see these elderly people at the end of their life, I see my parents in them. I cannot love on my own parents, so I love on my patients as if they were my family. I treat them in the way I would want people to treat me."

My mother was so touched that as she relayed the story to me, she had tears in her eyes. Some would say that this precious woman's job was unimportant, but this woman became the hands and feet of Jesus as she interacted with the sick and dying. Jesus said, "I tell you the truth, whatever you did for one of the least of these brothers of mine, you did for me" (Matt. 25:40).

When I was a wedding planner I often heard 1 Corinthians 13 recited in weddings:

> Love is patient, love is kind. It does not envy, it does not boast, it is not proud. It is not rude, it is not self-seeking, it is not easily angered, it keeps no record of wrongs. Love does not delight in evil but rejoices with

the truth. It always protects, always trusts, always hopes, always perseveres. Love never fails.

—1 Corinthians 13:4–8

This passage has become the "wedding passage," yet it is so much more. What it teaches goes far beyond how we are to treat a spouse. We have been commanded to love everyone, thus this verse is the guideline for how we should treat every person we come into contact with. Let's take a look at those qualities again:

- Love is patient.
- Love is kind.
- It does not envy.
- It does not boast.
- It is not proud.
- It is not rude.
- It is not self-seeking.
- It is not easily angered.
- It keeps no record of wrongs.
- Love does not delight in evil.
- It rejoices with the truth.
- It always protects.
- It always trusts.
- It always hopes.
- It always perseveres.

How many of us can say that we live those qualities out on a daily basis? I know I have a lot of work to do. I have missed the mark on most of these in some way in just the last forty-eight hours! According to God's definition of love, I do not always love my husband the way I should. I do not always love my family members as I should. I do not always love the person in the car in front of me who is driving way too slowly, the bookstore clerk who has ignored me for five minutes, or the neighbor who parked on my grass. Wow, loving people seems almost impossible. And it is, apart from the Lord.

LOVING PEOPLE HELPS US HEAL

Depression makes us so conscious of our own needs and our own pain that it limits our ability to truly want to meet others' needs before our own. Basically most depressed people become very selfish, not because they want to but because hurting people are often so depleted that they don't have a lot in reserve to give to others. I functioned in a self-focused manner when I was depressed. I was so needy that I couldn't even stop to see others' needs. I was so depleted that I looked to others to give me what I did not have. I desired others to serve me and to meet my needs first. But I was so wrong! Thank the Lord that He has changed my heart! I am here to tell you that *loving others is a very powerful way to receive healing for yourself.*

Anytime we serve others, the Lord promises to fill us with His power for the task. Serving others will pull us out of despair faster than anything else will. If you are experiencing the self-focus that comes from depression, you may not even recognize your selfish attitude, but ask the Lord to reveal to you whether or not you have put your needs above the needs of your brothers and sisters. Loving others and serving them will break this thought pattern so that it no longer has a hold on you. "There is no fear in love. But perfect love drives out fear.... And he has given us this command: Whoever loves God must also love his brother" (1 John 4:18, 21).

Besides setting us free, loving others will bless us as well. Many years ago, after I was married, my husband and I attended a nice church that had an active Sunday school class for young married couples. I was really hoping to develop friendships in that class, because I had been lonely since moving to a new city. I thought that since I was now in a Sunday school class, my lonely days would be over. I tried to become friends with several of the girls, and I hoped to be invited into their group of friends. But my phone didn't ring, and the invitations didn't come. I prayed and prayed, asking God to give me friends. Nothing happened. I felt left out and unwanted.

After a year of this I decided that if I wanted friends, I would have to be the one to initiate. I was nervous, but I picked up my phone and started doing the asking. I asked girls to come to dinner, to go shopping, to come over for game nights, and I also started calling them just to see how *they* were doing. Something magical happened. Over time I developed friendships. When Kevin and I changed churches, I did the same thing again. I initiated. Now I have almost more friendships than I can keep up with. I decided to be the one to bless others first, and I saw a huge response.

When my husband and I led singles' Bible-study groups, those first few weeks when no one knew each other were always a little tough on some people. I would watch some folks hang back, waiting for someone to come and talk to them first. In our first meeting I would always tell the group, "To make friends, you have to take the initiative to go up to others and show a genuine interest in them. Others are as nervous as you are. Find someone to reach out to and to bless, and you will find that building relationships will become easier." This is true in every situation, whether personal or business. When we look to bless others first, we will in turn be blessed. "For he who is least among you all—he is the greatest" (Luke 9:48). If you want to be a great friend to others, elevate them above yourself. And by the way, if you are single or lonely, if you put this verse into practice, people will be drawn to you. It works every time.

Jesus taught, "Seek first [the Father's] kingdom and his righteousness, and all these things will be given to you as well" (Matt. 6:33). God asks us to stop living for ourselves. He asks us to put His kingdom first, other people first, and *then* He will take care of our needs. The kingdom of God operates in stark contrast to the way the world operates. To be first in the kingdom of God, we have to decide to serve others (Mark 9:35).

One day as Jesus was teaching, a Pharisee who was an expert of the law asked Jesus, "Teacher, which is the greatest commandment in the Law?" (Matt. 22:36). Listen to what Jesus told him:

> Jesus replied: "'Love the Lord your God with all your heart and with all your soul and with all your mind.' This is the first and greatest commandment. And the second is like it: '*Love your neighbor as yourself.*' All the Law and the Prophets hang on these two commandments."
> —Matthew 22:37–40, emphasis added

Jesus was basically saying that the entire Old Testament came down to loving God and loving people. "So in everything, do to others what you would have them do to you, for this sums up the Law and the Prophets" (Matt. 7:12). Children in kindergarten are often taught that this is the Golden Rule. This law of God's is so important that it has found its way into secular teachings. You can call it the Golden Rule or you can call it God's law, but whatever you call it, put it into practice!

"Was not our ancestor Abraham considered righteous for what he did...? You see that his faith and his actions were working together, and *his faith was made complete by what he did....* You see that a person is justified by *what he does* and not by faith alone" (James 2:21–22, 24, emphasis added). Serving others makes our faith complete. As Solomon wrote, "I know that there is nothing better for men than to be happy and *do good* while they live" (Eccles. 3:12, emphasis added). Putting actions and deeds alongside our attitudes of faith gives our lives meaning and significance. Whenever you serve others, you will find that your own purpose is discovered.

HINDRANCES TO LOVING PEOPLE

Isolation keeps us from loving others.

Isolation is one condition that almost every depressed person needs to conquer in order to find complete freedom. Isolation is often a catalyst for depression, and it inhibits our ability to focus on and love others. Depression will tell us to isolate ourselves, to deal with things on our own and not let anyone in our world. Isolation has a pattern:

- Feeling isolated leads to being alone.

- Being alone leads to loneliness.

- Loneliness leads to hopelessness.

- Hopelessness is the definition of depression.

So what can we do to break this cycle? First, we need to consider whether we may have a tendency to isolate ourselves as a survival mechanism. Isolation can be external or internal.

A person who is internally isolated may be quite active and very social, but no one knows what is really going on inside the person. This was a perfect description of how I was when I was depressed. No one would have guessed that I was dying on the inside. I remained social, sought out things to keep me busy, and found it easy to talk with people. If anyone in the dorm yelled up, "Hey, I'm going out for ice cream, anyone want to come?", I was ready to jump in the car. I had the outside all taken care of, but inside me there was a great tornado raging.

The reason I was constantly busy with other people was not because I was a social butterfly but because I could not operate on my own. My anxiety was so high that I could not be content by myself. I literally *had* to be around other people because I would fall apart when I was by myself. I lived in a dorm full of girls, so I constantly operated in this unhealthy pattern. I spent most of my college years overextending myself, because I thought activity would crowd out my discontentment.

Of course, I didn't find peace in keeping busy. I only found peace when I was finally able to be content standing on my own two feet. If you suffer from internal isolation, you need to seek out contentment in the quiet times of your day. Let go of activity that crowds your life or that simply drowns out the noise of your anxiety. It is equally important that you let others in on what's happening in your heart. You need people to know what is really going on inside you. Use your prayer partner to help you. Decide to break the pattern of internal isolation today.

External isolation is the most obvious type of isolation.

Socialization is a normal part of developing in maturity and enjoying life, but when people isolate themselves externally, they withdraw from everything. They retract from friendships, from going places, from doing things with friends and family, and they constantly offer excuses as to why they cannot attend functions. Their homes become the place where they are comfortable, and they develop extreme anxiety when forced to be in social situations.

Several of my family members suffer from this type of isolation, and it is difficult to watch. No one can understand why the person chooses to withdraw, because they don't realize that there are much deeper issues at hand than not wanting to be around people. If you struggle with external isolation, make a decision to stay active and to get involved with people. Join a club, a sports team, or a Bible study, or spend more time around your family. The more you participate in social situations, the easier it will become for you.

Whether internal or external, isolation works to undermine our potential and our happiness. Isolation contributes to anxiety, which then creates fear. This fear keeps people from moving forward in life but at the same time makes enjoying the present very difficult. The Lord has overcome fear. He can heal us of our anxiety and fear and deliver us from isolation as we continue to walk in Him. Remember that depression, anxiety, and isolation assault our perception and attack our minds. Fight back through prayer, and keep your thoughts on the good things of the Lord.

We were never created to walk alone in this life. God put within us a desire to connect with others. This is a good desire and a healthy one. It is through this connection with people that we can minister, love, and be loved and cared for. Satan works to twist this desire for relationship and to use it to harm us instead. If our desire to connect with others gets messed up, our whole life can feel out of balance. Jesus always had His disciples around Him, and they enjoyed life and ministry together. We should seek to live full lives with rich friendships as well.

Anger keeps us from loving others.

"A patient man has great understanding, but a quick-tempered man displays folly" (Prov. 14:29). A lot of people walk through life in anger. Anger pushes other people away from us and makes them afraid to deal with us. People will never be honest with an angry person, because they are too afraid of the consequences. A person who is angry will never be able to develop meaningful and lasting relationships, because anger will get in the way of forming godly intimacy with others.

Anger can be expressed in several ways. It is not always communicated in the form of shouting or manipulation. Anger can keep as quiet as a mouse at times. Passive-aggressive people will usually keep silent until they can take no more, and when their anger comes out, it can be through getting back at a person, giving someone the silent treatment, or trying to control people. No matter how we express unhealthy anger, we need to recognize that this behavior will keep us from God's best for our lives and will destroy our relationships.

Just as with our other mind-sets, being angry is a choice. We must choose how to handle our emotions. When something does not go your way, is your first reaction one of anger? Have people told you that you are passive aggressive or that you have an anger issue? Deal with any anger you have and ask God for a new heart. We cannot love others when we carry around an angry attitude.

A self-serving attitude keeps us from loving others.

"An argument started among the disciples as to which of them would be the greatest" (Luke 9:46). The disciples actually had an argument about this! This may sound silly to us as we read the Book of Luke—but how far are we from having this mind-set?

I hear conversations at work all the time that sound a whole lot like this one that the disciples had, each person trying to prove his value to the company. There is something rebellious in each one of us that wants the attention, or the limelight, if you will. We want to be the first to get out of the busy parking lot, the first one to sign up as homeroom mom, the first to buy the newest style of purse. We think greatness is achieved when we are somehow first, better, or getting the most attention.

Having a self-serving mind-set will always keep us from putting others' needs before our own. If we function with a "me first" attitude, we will never truly love others or please the Lord. We certainly cannot minister to people if we are concerned only about ourselves. Serving others can be uncomfortable. It can cause us extra work and be very tiring. Unfortunately we cannot get out of having a servant's heart just because it looks too difficult. As disciples of the Lord, we must learn how to serve others with joy. Loving ourselves, loving God, and loving others are all integral parts of finding our own freedom from depression.

Satan's ultimate purpose for depression in a Christian's life is to keep us from ever reaching our full potential in Christ. And you do have amazing potential! The Pharisees once asked Jesus when the kingdom of God would come, and Jesus replied by saying, "The kingdom of God is within you" (Luke 17:21). If you are a Christian, the kingdom of God is within *you*. Allow this mighty river of life to heal you, fill you, and teach you.

To God be the glory for your healing. Amen.

Dig Deeper
---

1. How do we "remain in the Lord"?

2. Why is love greater than faith or hope?

3. Take another look at the "Love is..." passage (1 Cor. 13:4–8). In which areas do you need to focus on better loving people?

4. What type of isolation might you struggle with? How can you work to get free of this?

5. Why does God put so much focus on us serving others?

Assignments

Exercise 1: Find ways to serve others and meet their needs.

Serving people is a blessing and will quickly pull you out of your own problems and toward the joy that comes from meeting others' needs. Decide how you are going to start serving others and write down your ideas. You could serve through doing outreach in your city, feeding and clothing the less fortunate, teaching a kids' Sunday school class, taking care of chores for an elderly neighbor, or going out of your way to call someone each week who is hurting and needs encouragement. Think about how you can use your talents and gifts to help others. Decide to start serving others on a regular basis, and watch your heart fill up with the love of God.

Exercise 2: Activate the Golden Rule in your life.

You will see an immediate response when you begin to look for ways to treat others as you would want to be treated. Look the salesperson in the eye. Call people by name. Say thank you more often. Open the door for people. Put merchandise back in its place instead of leaving it for someone else to put away. Take your shopping cart back to where you got it. You will find that when you are actively looking for ways to be a blessing, you will start living a true lifestyle of excellence. You will also see a great change in your family as you activate the Golden Rule within your home.

Prayer time

> *Lord, teach me how to put others before myself. Show me how to remain in You all day long. Pour love for others into my heart, and help me to see people as You see them. Help me to serve others as if I was serving You. Change my attitude toward the people around me. Let me see that it is a privilege to minister to people through my words and my actions. Release me from any type of isolation that would keep me from Your best for my life. Help me to treat others as I would want to be treated. In Jesus's name, amen.*

Conclusion

LOOKING FORWARD

Forget the former things; do not dwell on the
past. See, I am doing a new thing! Now it springs
up; do you not perceive it? I am making a way
in the desert and streams in the wasteland.
—*Isaiah 43:18–19*

HEALING COMES IN many forms. In Mark 7:33 Jesus met a deaf man, and He "put his fingers into the man's ears. Then he spit and touched the man's tongue." That is certainly an unusual approach to healing, isn't it? In John 9:6 Jesus used mud and saliva to heal a blind man, and then in Mark 10 He healed a blind man simply by saying, "Your faith has healed you" (v. 52). Why did Jesus heal people in so many ways? I believe He wanted to let us know, "Look, I often don't work the same way twice. There is not a formula or graph that can predict My ways. I minister to each person differently because I know their needs, and I have a plan for each of My children."

I have heard hundreds of healing stories, and no two are the same. God is both creative and particular in how He chooses to deal with each one of us. What we cannot do is begin to despise the way God chooses to work within us when He doesn't meet our needs the way we think He should. It's too easy to look at another's path to healing and expect our steps to follow those footprints exactly. When our progress seems to lag behind or stop all together for a season, we shouldn't assume that God has stopped His healing work. In fact, it is most often when we cannot see Him working that break-through is near.

It's a trap to compare yourself to others, and it brings about contempt in your own heart. We are all walking out our own journeys with the Lord. The story I have to tell will be different from yours. If you worked through this book in a small-group setting, your testimony will be different from the others in the group. The beauty of the gospel is that Jesus has an individual relationship with each of us, so our paths to freedom will be tailored to meet our own needs.

As we end our study together, I want to leave you with a few final thoughts about the journey to healing.

God has a time for all things.

Habakkuk 2:3 says, "For the revelation awaits an appointed time.... Though it linger, wait for it; it will certainly come and will not delay." One of the most difficult aspects of the Christian walk is waiting for the Lord to fulfill a promise. Many saints give up when it looks like nothing is happening, or they get so discouraged that their faith falls apart. Fight the urge to throw in the towel when your timing and God's timing aren't in step.

I almost gave up on being involved in ministry because after longing for years to teach, the doors just were not opening. I remember telling God how disappointed I was, and for several years I thought my dream was totally dead. Seven years later God did open the door for me to minister, and I have stepped through without hesitation. God had a specific *time* for me, though at one point it sure didn't feel like I would ever minister the gospel. I also remember wondering if I would ever gain freedom from depression. But again God had a specific *time* for my total healing, and in 2001, right before I met my husband, I found the freedom I had been praying for.

The Lord has a set time for you as well, a time for each of your dreams to come to pass and a time for your healing to come to fruition. Everyone wants healing in the immediate moment, but I have to say that most people's healing from depression comes through a process, and this process takes time. If you complete this study and say to yourself, "I am nowhere close to being totally healed," don't assume the Lord will not bring radical healing in your life.

Remember what I said in chapters 1 and 2 about giving God what you cannot control? It takes great faith to trust God with your healing but even greater faith to trust Him with the *timing* of that healing. Use this book as a starting point for your journey rather than as a marker of the end. As long as you keep moving forward, you will reach the finish line the Lord has drawn for you. Don't measure your spiritual success by where you think you should be right now but by how close you walk with Jesus. That is the truest measure of spiritual wealth, and it is your close walk with Jesus that will ultimately bring the healing you desire.

Obey what God tells you to do.

Second John 1:6 tells us, "And this is love: that we walk in obedience." I cannot stress often enough how doing everything the Lord tells you to do will change your life and bring powerful healing to your soul. I mentioned earlier in the book the importance of taking responsibility for the things you have the ability to control. Whatever the Lord has spoken to you to do during this study, do it! Don't leave these promptings undone because your path to healing is dependent on your willingness to work *with* the Holy Spirit. He can't and won't do all the work for you.

We always have a role to play in anything the Lord does in our lives. We can either partner with Him and allow Him to work in us, or we can refuse His leadership. Honestly there are certain things the Lord will ask you to do that you simply will not want to do. You will come up with excuses and tell yourself that surely there is another way. You will want to put off obeying God or tell yourself you did not hear God's voice at all.

But when the Lord speaks to you, please do not ignore His voice. Ignoring His voice will only prolong your problems and keep you going around the same mountain over and over. For example, if you need to forgive someone, don't hold back. Your destiny will be unlocked as you learn to hear and *obey*. Now is the time to do what you have learned, and the most precious nuggets you can take from this book are the things that the Lord has specifically spoken to you to do. Don't delay. Obedience will walk you to the door of freedom.

Appreciate what the Lord has done for you already.

Psalm 105:1–2 says, "Give thanks to the LORD, call on his name; make known among the nations what he has done. Sing to him, sing praise to him; tell of all his wonderful acts." It's so easy to constantly look ahead and pine for the *next* in our life, but it is wise to acknowledge the large (and the small) miracles we experience in the moment. Now is a wonderful time to pause and thank the Lord for what He has already accomplished just since you began reading this book. In fact, make a list and celebrate the victories.

I learned the value of remembrance in just the last couple of years. The Israelites had been wandering in the wilderness for forty years when they finally began heading toward the Promised Land. In their way was one huge obstacle: the Jordan River. Joshua told the people the Lord would do an amazing thing—and He certainly did. He caused the river to part so the Israelites could walk across on dry land. After they crossed over, the Lord told Joshua to have one man from each of the twelve tribes carry a rock from the middle of the Jordan and place the stones in their camp to serve as a sign (Josh. 4:6) and memorial (v. 7) of the miracle the Lord had done.

After I read this account in Joshua 4, I decided that I too needed stones of remembrance in my life. If you take a look at my calendar, you'll see that I have special dates highlighted, each representing a stone of remembrance in my life. When those dates roll around each year, my husband and I celebrate them and mark in our life what the Lord did for us. One of those dates is April 10, the day I received a call from Charisma House offering me a publishing deal for the book you are now reading.

I don't honor that day because I scored a book offer, but because on that day I saw how God could use my brother's tragic death to shake hell and honor heaven. And every April 10 from now until I see Jesus I will thank Him that He was able to take what Satan meant for harm and use it to touch lives and further His kingdom.

You too need to erect stones of remembrance in your own life when you experience the miraculous, the beautiful, and the answers to your prayers. Celebrate your breakthroughs, no matter how large or small, for each one is a point at which heaven touched earth and created a supernatural result in your life. Look for stones from the "Jordan Rivers" God has brought you across, and decide to remember God's mighty hand in your life. These stones of remembrance will become precious to you and to Jesus when you honor them. What has God done for you as you have studied this book? It's time to erect a stone of remembrance.

Be ready for a fight.

"Your enemy the devil prowls around like a roaring lion looking for someone to devour" (1 Pet. 5:8). The Christian life is a battleground, and I wouldn't love you if I didn't tell you that after you find healing in any area of your life, Satan will come knocking, trying to convince you that you were not really healed. In fact, go ahead and expect it. He will look for any way back into your life to play the same games he once tortured you with. Instead of being surprised by Satan's attacks, be ready. Know in advance what you will do if Satan tries to convince you that anything God revealed to you through this book isn't true.

When he tells you that God doesn't care, that healing is not for you, that it's OK to withhold forgiveness, that God loves others more than you, get ready for a fight—and fight to win, my friend. We are overcomers by the blood of the Lamb and the word of our testimony (Rev. 12:11). Our power comes through Jesus, and we are to trust, obey, and stand on the Word of God. When my brother passed away, I had been free from depression and anxiety for years. But in that tragic moment the door to depression and anxiety swung open. Satan brought an army of evil to try to convince me that my heart was too weak to stay free and that I would be pulled down into the pit of despair once more.

For several days I experienced the nightmare of depression and anxiety all over again. I confused it with grief, so I didn't shut it out at first. But a moment of clarity came from the Holy Spirit, and I realized that grief and depression were two separate things. I had to embrace grief, but I had to battle against depression and anxiety like my life depended on it.

I almost fell for Satan's trick, but thank the Lord I picked up my sword and fought with the truth of God's Word. I did embrace my grief, and at the same time I decided that anxiety and depression had no place in my life, no matter what had happened. And as quickly as it came, the depression left. I know if I had been passive, I might not have remained free. But because I knew what to do in the heat of the battle, I was victorious. You need to be ready for a fight and know that when God sets you free in any area of your life, it is His intention that you *stay* free.

Seek more help if you need it.

The writer of Ecclesiastes said, "If one falls down, his friend can help him up. But pity the man who falls and has no one to help him up!" (Eccles. 4:10). Fear keeps so many people from asking for help. If you need more help from this point, then seek it out. Help is not going to just fall out of the sky. Do some research to find some great Christian counselors in your city. Seek out groups that will support your healing process, and keep in touch with your prayer partner even after you have finished working through this book.

If you need daily help to get better, then be brave and enter into a program that can give you the assistance you need to get healthy. On my author website, www.jennyswindall.com, I have some great resource links that you may find helpful. Whatever you do, don't go this alone, and don't let fear rob you of going forward to victory. Now is the time to be fearless in pressing toward wholeness.

Let's pray together, thanking God for what He has done and what He will continue to do in your life.

Thank You, Lord, for all that You have spoken to me and have done within my heart as I have worked through this book. Please continue to stir within me the waters of healing so I may come to a place of total freedom in You. Prepare me for the days ahead and to do battle against the enemy. Cover me with Your protection and hide me away in You. I pray that everything You have begun in me, You will bring to completion. Teach me everything I need to know to walk out what I have learned, and touch my mind so that my thoughts will honor You. Thank You for breaking the chains of depression off my life and for doing a great work in me. Give me boldness so that I can share my story to encourage others. In Jesus's name, amen.

NOTES

Chapter 1—The Great Thief

1. Centers for Disease Control and Prevention, "Antidepressant Use in Persons Aged 12 and Over: United States, 2005–2008," October 2011, http://www.cdc.gov/nchs/data/databriefs/db76.htm (accessed February 13, 2013).

2. Marie Stagnitti, "Antidepressant Use in the U.S. Civilian Noninsitutionalized Population, 2002" Medical Expenditure Panel, Agency for Healthcare Research and Quality, http://meps.ahrq.gov/data_files/publications/st77/stat77.pdf (accessed February 28, 2013).

Chapter 3—Reintroduce Hope

1. Trent C. Butler, s.v. "hope," *Holman Bible Dictionary* (Nashville: Broadman & Holman, 1991), http://www.studylight.org/dic/hbd/view.cgi?n =2841 (accessed February 13, 2013).

2. Evan Thomas, "A Good Day to Die," *New York Times*, November 12, 2010, http://www.nytimes.com/2010/11/14/books/review/Thomas-t.html?_r=1& (accessed February 28, 2013); Thomas Powers, *The Killing of Crazy Horse* (New York: Vintage Books, 2010), 339, 414.

Chapter 5—Take a Moral Inventory

1. Harry Gersh, *Talmud: Law and Commentary* (Springfield, NJ: Behrman House, 1986), 5–7; Mendy Hecht, "The 613 Commandments," http://www.chabad.org/library/article_cdo/aid/756399/jewish/The-613 -Commandments.htm (accessed February 28, 2013).

Chapter 6—Forgive Those Who Have Hurt You

1. John Wesley, John Wesley's Explanatory Notes on Luke 6:38, http://www.christnotes.org/commentary.php?b=42&c=6&com=wes (accessed February 14, 2013).

Chapter 7—Find Your Identity in Christ

1. "Fighting Back Against Identity Theft," Federal Trade Commission, http://www.ftc.gov/bcp/edu/pubs/consumer/idtheft/idt06.pdf (accessed February 21, 2013).

Chapter 9—Seek God's Will

1. David Pawson, *Unlocking the Bible* (Travelers Rest, SC: True Potential Publishing, 2009), http://www.pawsonbooks.com/blog/week-107-ecclesiastes -part-4 (accessed February 21, 2013).

ABOUT THE AUTHOR

Jenny Swindall earned a bachelor of science degree in microbiology from Auburn University, which led to a career in the pharmaceutical industry. She later transitioned into the specialized market of biologic clinical sales and has since received national sales awards in that field.

Jenny and her husband, Kevin, began ministering after leading a small group Bible study with just six people in their living room. The group quickly grew so large that they had to finish their basement and designate parking attendants in the neighborhood to accommodate the crowd. Known for their powerful storytelling and insightful biblical teaching, Jenny and her husband have ministered to hundreds in their hometown of Birmingham, Alabama.

Freedom From Depression was birthed out of Jenny's own struggle and triumph over depression. After losing her brother to suicide, Jenny wrote *Freedom From Depression* as a resource for others seeking total healing from the bondage of depression.

When not leading Bible studies, Jenny and Kevin can often be found playing with their three big rescue dogs, hanging out with their families, and completing projects around the house. When Jenny isn't busy writing, her other hobby is designing jewelry. You can find her designs at www.jelizabeth.com.

Visit Jenny's website at www.jennyswindall.com to access:

- Additional resources on healing from depression
- Videos related to the chapters
- Tools to begin your own Freedom From Depression small group
- A free app just for you!